Breakthroughs

An Integrated Advanced English Program

Breakthroughs

AN INTEGRATED ADVANCED ENGLISH PROGRAM

Marina Engelking   **Gloria McPherson-Ramirez**

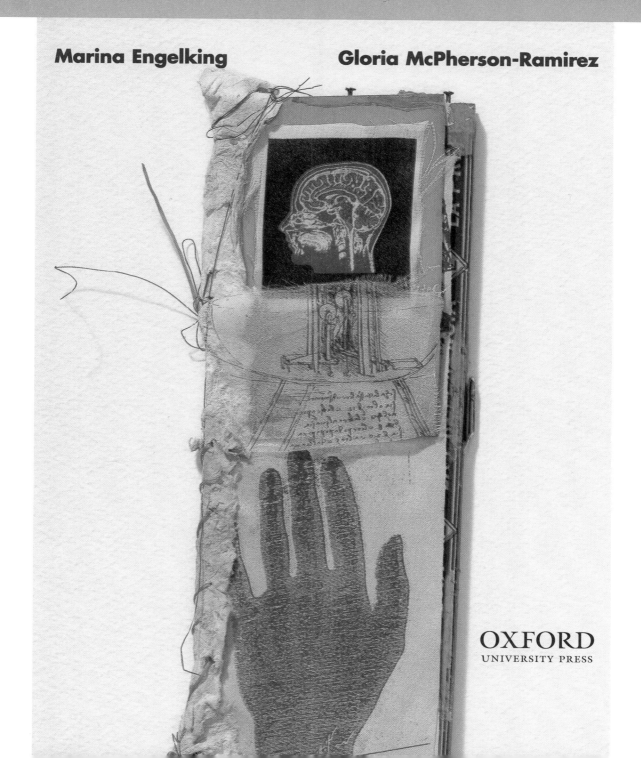

OXFORD
UNIVERSITY PRESS

OXFORD
UNIVERSITY PRESS

70 Wynford Drive, Don Mills, Ontario M3C 1J9
www.oup.com/ca

Oxford University Press is a department of the University of Oxford.
It furthers the University's objective of excellence in research, scholarship,
and education by publishing worldwide in

Oxford New York

Auckland Bangkok Buenos Aires Cape Town Chennai
Dar es Salaam Delhi Hong Kong Istanbul Karachi Kolkata
Kuala Lumpur Madrid Melbourne Mexico City Mumbai Nairobi
São Paulo Shanghai Taipei Tokyo Toronto

Oxford is a trade mark of Oxford University Press
in the UK and in certain other countries

Published in Canada
by Oxford University Press

Canadian Cataloguing in Publication Data
Engelking, Marina, 1959-
          Breakthroughs: an integrated advanced English program

ISBN 0-19-541172-2

1. English language.   I. McPherson-Ramirez, Gloria, 1963- .
II. Title.

PE1112.E54 1997   428   C97-932170-0

Since this page cannot accommodate all copyright notices, page v
constitutes an extension of the copyright page.

Cover art: Susan Leopold
Cover & interior design: Heather Delfino
Illustrators: Kathryn Adams, Raffi Anderian, Giovannina Colalillo,
Michael Custode, Heather Delfino, Robert Johannsen, Susan Leopold,
Colin McRae (Caterpillar Graphics), Brett Miller, Caroline Price,
Sue Todd, Brenda Weeks, Janet Wilson, Farida Zaman, Leon Zernitsky

This book is printed on permanent (acid-free) paper ∞.
Printed in Canada

5 - 03 02

Speaking	Writing (including Workbook)	Vocabulary	Grammar
– giving detailed instructions on the phone – presenting a newscast – presenting a natural disaster emergency plan – discussing complex environmental issues	Focus: Prewriting techniques, topic sentences (WB) Activities: newspaper report, journal article, legend (SB)	– categorizing words – identifying their grammatical functions – completing proverbs using meaning and rhyme – using nature images in daily speech	<u>Passive Voice</u> – Grammar in Use: writing newspaper headlines, writing a journal article
– retelling an incident from different characters' perspectives – discussing paranormal issues – describing events	Focus: Narrative paragraphs (WB) Activities: paragraph about an unexplained event, letter retelling an account, fictional story written in the round (SB)	– matching words with meanings (dictionary work) – prefixes and meaning	<u>Reported Speech (Statements and Questions)</u> – Grammar in Use: relating accounts of the supernatural orally and retelling events and opinions
– formulating questions based on responses – role playing a telephone conversation – presenting a detailed description of a place – discussing complex issues	Focus: Descriptive paragraphs (WB) Activities: journal entry, descriptive essay, dialogue (SB)	– brainstorming precise descriptive words – unscrambling adjectives from context – matching formal and less formal descriptive phrases – word choice	<u>Adjective Order in Descriptions</u> – Grammar in Use: writing a descriptive paragraph, postcard, or description from a photograph <u>Relative Clauses</u> – Grammar in Use: writing sentence clues for an object that teammates must identify
– brainstorming and sharing information – presenting arguments and paraphrasing	Focus: Comparison/Contrast paragraphs (WB) Activities: comparison/contrast paragraphs, anecdote, journal entry, brochure (SB)	– idioms associated with communication – matching words with meanings and prepositions	<u>Conjunctions and Prepositions of Contrast/Transition Words and Phrases of Contrast</u> – Grammar in Use: writing a comparison/contrast essay, writing contrastive sentences
– developing and presenting a commercial – expressing opinions, agreement, and disagreement	Focus: Expository paragraphs (WB) Activities: brochure, letter of inquiry, expository paragraph, newsletter (SB)	– noun + preposition collocations – common scientific roots	<u>Noun Clauses</u> – Grammar in Use: writing sentences with noun clauses, panel discussion

Speaking	Writing (including Workbook)	Vocabulary	Grammar
- presenting arguments and opinions in a debate - presenting a speech - problem-solving in a group	Focus: Cause and Effect paragraphs (WB) Activities: summary, explanatory paragraph, biography (SB)	- using words associated with intelligence - word puzzle using pronunciation, meaning, and word form clues - phrasal verbs	"If "Statements (Conditionals) - Grammar in Use: exploring options and giving advice Modals - Grammar in Use: solving a riddle
- role playing a commercial - presenting a super-hero character	Focus: Essay Basics (outlines, structure, thesis statements) (WB) Activities: essays, movie/television review, "what happens next" story continuation, TV episode (SB)	- using picture and letter clues to decipher words - matching words and meaning - crossword puzzle	To + Base Verbals - Grammar in Use: describing phobias
- retelling a story - practising intonation and stress - teaching a new game - debating a topic - conducting a survey	Focus: Introductory paragraphs (WB) Activities: paragraph supporting an opinion, comparison/contrast essay (SB)	- sports idioms (crossword) - sounding out words from clues (vanity licence plates) - onomatopoeic words	Base + ing Verbals - Grammar in Use: describing sports Base + ing Verbals (Gerunds) vs. Infinitives - Grammar in Use: Three Strikes- You're Out game
- compiling and discussing the results of a questionnaire - committee work and recommendations - presenting an interview	Focus: Concluding paragraphs (WB) Activities: newspaper editorial, summary, essay, outline for a report (SB)	- matching words and meanings from context - word forms - suffixes and meaning	Base + d/t/n Verbals - Grammar in Use: writing sentences using the verbals based on a paragraph
- using rhyme and meaning to match beginnings and endings of nursery rhymes - presenting a time capsule - telling a story - discussing personal "circles of life"	Focus: Narrative/Descriptive essays (WB) Activities: children's story, prose poem, narrative essay (SB)	-deducing meaning from context -word forms -formality register (writing informal equivalents for formal words)	Tense Review - Grammar in Use: panel discussion

Introduction

Welcome to *Breakthroughs,* a stimulating, theme-based advanced English language program for young adults and adults. This communicative, integrated-skills program takes you on a journey of discovery through the landscape of English, developing skills in reading, writing, listening, and speaking. Unlike many other language texts which focus primarily on controlled practice and communicative activities, this program encourages you to "break through" the confines of traditional approaches to assimilate your knowledge and skills so that you can express critical thought in English.

Theories about how best to develop language skills abound in the academic literature. We believe that the key to learning any subject successfully lies in motivation. We have built the *Breakthroughs* program around themes that are not only current and relevant, but also interesting and thought-provoking. Each unit begins with a creative visual, quiz, puzzle, or discussion activity that introduces the unit theme and invites you to participate actively in the learning process. A variety of provocative and creative individual, pair, team, and class exercises in the four skill areas then guide you through controlled practice and communicative activities with a focus on developing critical thinking skills.

The reading activities focus on valuable skills such as skimming, scanning, predicting, inferring, and reading charts and graphs, and are built around readings taken from various sources including literature, newspapers, journals, magazines, and the Internet. Fun and inspiring listening activities include political speeches, scientific interviews, poetry, and popular songs. The writing activities in each unit offer practice in functional and academic writing from letters, brochures, advertisements, and journal articles to summaries, paragraphs, and essays for specific purposes. A complete academic writing program is built into the accompanying student Workbook. *Breakthroughs* also places a strong emphasis on developing effective speaking skills. Lively speaking activities range from participating in debates, presenting sales pitches and panel discussions, and giving oral presentations to practising telephone conversations, and a variety of informal and formal conversations found in daily life. In addition to developing the more traditional language skills, *Breakthroughs* stresses the expression of higher level thinking skills. While the program includes common themes such as Food, the perspective offered on each theme challenges you to think beyond the common treatment of these themes, offering real "food for thought." Many activities have a One Step Beyond component, a unique feature of this text, which encourages you to synthesize and apply your knowledge to make inferences. These sections also act as a springboard to addressing issues on a broader, more sophisticated level.

While the aim of *Breakthroughs* is to build communicative competence at an advanced level, vocabulary building and grammar, two areas often neglected in other advanced English texts, are also included. You not only build your vocabulary, but learn strategies that will allow you to continue to broaden your word power beyond the scope of this text. The Grammar Focus in each unit provides clear explanations and useful exercises that lead you to communicate effectively using standard English grammar. Finally, each unit ends with a Unit Reflection, an activity that serves to summarize the unit and that prompts you to integrate and apply the knowledge and skills you have practised. Although the units were designed to stand alone, we suggest following them in sequence to build on the grammar components of the Student Book and the writing program in the accompanying Workbook.

A student Workbook, an audio cassette, and a Teacher's Book accompany the *Breakthroughs* student text. Ideal for homework, the Workbook provides further practice in and expansion of concepts learned in the Student Book, and includes an academic writing program that guides you through the writing process from pre-writing tasks to paragraph and essay writing for various rhetorical modes. A complete answer key for all activities is provided. The audio cassette program offers important practice in listening and comprehension skills with an emphasis on developing effective listening strategies. The Teacher's Book goes beyond the traditional teacher's manual to include not only a complete answer key to the Student Book activities and the tapescript of all listening material on the audio cassette, but suggestions on introducing, varying, and expanding activities in both the Student Book and Workbook. One Step Ahead boxes address points a teacher should consider before introducing specific activities. For convenience, the Teacher's Book also includes photocopiable unit quizzes, a mid-term and final test, and various structured and communicative activities such as grammar and vocabulary games, and role-plays.

Journeying through the landscape of English is challenging and exciting. With the *Breakthroughs* Advanced English Program, we believe your journey will be encouraging, provocative, and enjoyable.

Marina Engelking
Gloria McPherson-Ramirez

Acknowledgements

A project of this scope is only possible through the successful collaboration of a team of skilled and dedicated professionals. We feel privileged to have worked with the supportive professionals at Oxford University Press, Canada and would like to thank the following people for their help and guidance in this monumental task. We were very fortunate to have been assigned a magnificent editor, Monica Schwalbe, whose patience, diplomacy, dedication, and high standards of excellence guided us through the various stages of production. A special thanks to Robert Doyle whose vision brought this team together and whose encouragement and enthusiasm were welcomed throughout the past year and a half. We are proud of the work Heather Delfino did to make this book come alive visually. Our thanks also to those who reviewed and pilot-tested our materials; your comments were invaluable. It has been a mutually rewarding and positive experience, both professionally and personally, to have worked in partnership with a respected colleague and friend, to create this final product.

I would especially like to thank my family for their endless love and patience. A warm thanks to my parents, Helga and Otto Reiss, who have supported and encouraged me throughout my life. Loving thanks also to my husband, Peter, and my sons, Nicholas and Christopher, my guiding lights and inspiration.

Marina Engelking

No project of this magnitude is possible without the loving support of one's family. I would like to thank my husband Henry and sons Martin and Jamie for their patience and inspiration; my parents Jack and Jean McPherson and in-laws Tulio and Ana Ramirez for their assistance and encouragement.

Gloria McPherson-Ramirez

Unit 1

The Calm Before the Storm

DISCUSSION

1. Match the natural disasters in the pictures with the appropriate newspaper headlines. Describe similar disasters that you are aware of.

2. Natural occurrences such as earthquakes, volcanoes, tornadoes, and floods have been around since the beginning of time. What makes these occurrences "disasters?"

3. With current advances in technology, why are we still unable to predict natural disasters accurately and prevent the resulting deaths?

Houses Destroyed as Earthquake Hits

RESIDENTS TERRORIZED BY SPECTACULAR TORNADO

Survivors Plucked to Safety by Helicopter

VILLAGE DEMOLISHED AS HURRICANE BLASTS COAST

Fires Ignited as Lightning Strikes

Would you survive?

Try the following quiz to determine your chances of surviving natural disasters. Then check your answers below and see how you scored.

1. If you are outdoors when an earthquake occurs, you should avoid trees, overpasses, and elevated expressways. **T / F**

2. If you are indoors during an earthquake, you should stay close to an outside door or window. **T / F**

3. Walking through floodwater that is below your knees is safe. **T / F**

4. If mobile homes are tied down securely, they are safe during a hurricane. **T / F**

5. Large hail, clouds of debris, and a roaring noise are all tornado danger signs. **T / F**

6. If you are in school when there is a tornado warning, it is safer to gather in the cafeteria than in an inner hallway. **T / F**

7. If you are close enough to see a tsunami, you are too close to escape it. **T / F**

8. If you are evacuating an area because of a volcanic eruption, you should wear a long-sleeved shirt, pants, eye goggles, and a dust mask. **T / F**

9. If you are in an open area and your hair stands on end, lightning is about to strike. **T / F**

10. During a lightning storm, it is safer to stand under a single tree in the open than a bunch of trees in the woods. **T / F**

Answers 1.T 2.F 3.F 4.F 5.T 6.F 7.T 8.T 9.T 10.F

If you scored:

10   You will lead others to safety if a disaster occurs.

8-9   Your knowledge will save your life.

6-7   You will probably survive if you follow your instincts.

4-5   Luck will play a large part in your survival.

1-3   Make sure you are always with a "10" – it's your only hope!

Vocabulary 1

1. Below are a number of words associated with natural disasters. Use your dictionary to check the meanings of any words you are not familiar with, and then copy the chart below and write the words in the appropriate columns.

epicentre	aftershocks	fissures
trembling	torrential rain	eye
eruption	poisonous gases	spew
lava	floodwater	twister
funnel	whiteout	blinding
deluge		

Earthquake	Hurricane	Volcano

Flood	Tornado	Blizzard

2. Identify whether the vocabulary words are nouns, verbs, or adjectives and use them to write sentences describing natural disasters.

> EXAMPLE: Aftershocks could be felt for days after the main quake.

Reading 1

You will read an extract from the *Bulletin of the American Meteorological Society.* The extract is an official news report based on a presentation made to the Symposium (conference) on the International Decade for Natural Disaster Reduction.

Before You Read

Work in pairs to discuss the following questions.

1. Meteorology is the scientific study of weather conditions, particularly their causes. Why is this an important field and how does it impact on your daily life?

2. What natural disasters are common in your native country? How do you prepare for them?

3. Approximately how many people do you think are killed by natural disasters each year?

Scanning

Quickly scan the text to find the following information.

1. When did disaster strike in Bangladesh?

2. Where were the wildfires located?

3. What is the world population expected to be by the middle of the next century?

4. How many people were killed by flood and by famine?

5. Working in pairs, find these words in the reading and match them with their definitions below. Use the context of the reading to determine the definitions. Then write a sentence for each word showing its meaning.

exacerbate	recurring	droughts
unprecedented	perennial	scourge
propagation	havoc	adversely
menaced		

a) to make worse

b) unfavourably

c) happening again and again

d) something that causes great suffering

e) never having occurred before

f) occurring every year

g) threatened

h) great destruction or disorder

i) long periods of time with little or no rain

j) spreading

Bulletin on the International Decade for Natural Disaster Reduction

Natural disasters have menaced humankind since the start of history. Millions of lives have been lost in the countless cyclones, recurring earthquakes, frequent floods, droughts, and other extreme events that hit the globe repeatedly.
5 Suffering, hardship, damage to property, and loss of livelihood feature all too frequently in the aftermath of such natural disasters.

Certainly, the unprecedented American Midwest flood of July/August 1993 figures prominently among these.
10 Floods also devastated a number of countries in western Europe in late 1993 and early 1994. At the same time droughts have persisted in many parts of Africa. The perennial scourge of tropical cyclones has brought havoc in the usual areas, and that of April 1991 in Bangladesh is
15 most notable. There was also the Mount Pinatubo eruption, whose effect in the atmosphere and in the directly affected areas is still being felt. Earthquakes such as those that hit India recently have also caused widespread suffering. There have been dramatic wildfires in
20 California and Australia whose uncontrolled propagation was aided by strong hot winds.

Probably more than three million people have been killed over the last 25 years by natural disasters, while a further one billion people have been adversely affected in
25 some way. (With a rapidly rising world population, expected to reach 10 billion by the middle of the next century, there will be a far larger target for natural disasters than today.) In addition, the pressure of population on land resources will demand that many more people must
30 live and work where the risks of disasters are highest: for instance, in river valleys and on coastal plains.

Changing climate is also a major concern for the future. A rising sea level will exacerbate the risk for the coastal populations as well as affect freshwater availability, while
35 shifts in the major climate belts may expose some communities to new hazards. Concern is also growing that, while some natural disasters are being amplified inadvertently by human activities (for example, deforestation of mountainous areas intensifying floods) others may
40 trigger environmental emergencies (for example, an earthquake resulting in radioactive or chemical releases to the atmosphere). In these circumstances, the arguments for improving the capabilities of the nations of the world to combat natural disasters are compelling.

Table 1 1967-1991: Total number of people killed by each type of natural disaster	
Type	**Number Killed**
a) Weather Events	
Cyclone	846 240
Hurricane	15 139
Typhoon	34 684
Flood	304 870
Storm	54 500
High wind	13 904
Cold and heat wave	4 926
Drought	1 333 728
b) Associated with Weather Events	
Avalanche	1 237
Landslide	41 992
Fire	81 970
Insect infestation	0
Famine	605 832
Food shortage	252
Epidemic	124 338
c) Geological	
Earthquake	646 307
Volcano	27 642
Tsunami	6 390

About 3.5 million people were killed by meteorological and hydrological events.

Reading for Information

Now read the text and find the answers to these questions.

1. There are six natural disasters discussed. What are they?
2. Where are risks of disasters greatest?
3. What natural hazards do we face in the future and why?
4. What type of natural disaster killed the most people from 1967–1991?
5. How many deaths have insect infestations caused? Could there be indirect deaths as a result of these infestations?

For Discussion

In teams of three or four, discuss the following.

1. Choose a suitable title for the reading from these suggestions:
   a) The Awesome Power of Nature
   b) Natural Killers
   c) The World Indefensible Against Nature
   d) People Vs. Nature
   e) The Human Cost of Natural Disasters

2. Governments spend billions of dollars compensating people who have lost their homes due to natural disasters. Should there be restrictions on where people can build houses?
3. What steps can we take to limit the impact of natural disturbances?
4. Where do you think the safest place is to live in the world (the place with the fewest natural disasters)? Why?

One Step Beyond

What human activities may be drastically affecting the environment and contributing to natural disasters?

ACID RAIN

Grammar Focus 1

PASSIVE VOICE

There are two ways to construct a sentence with very different effects.

ACTIVE:

subject (agent)	verb	object (receiver of action)

<u>Natural disasters</u> <u>have menaced</u> <u>humankind</u> since the start of history.

PASSIVE:

subject (receiver of action)	passive verb form	object of "by" phrase (agent)

<u>Humankind</u> <u>has been menaced</u> by <u>natural disasters</u> since the start of history.

Both of these sentences contain the same information. However, each sentence places the emphasis on a different aspect of that information. Which part of each sentence is being emphasized?

1. Form

In general we prefer to use the active voice; however, in certain circumstances, the passive is preferable. The passive voice puts more emphasis on the event than the doer (agent). Note the following when forming the passive voice:

- Only active sentences that contain an object may be put in the passive voice.

- The object of the active sentence becomes the subject of the passive sentence. The subject of the active sentence becomes the object of the "by" phrase.

- To form a passive sentence, we put the verb *be* in the same tense as the active verb and add the past participle of the active verb.

ACTIVE: Paramedics *carried* the injured to safety.
     verb (simple past tense)

PASSIVE: The injured *were carried* to safety by paramedics.
     verb *be* in simple past tense + past participle

Exercise A

Identify the subject (agent) and the object (receiver of the action) in the following sentences. Some sentences may not have an object. Determine if the sentences can be changed to the passive voice and then rewrite them.

EXAMPLE: Forest fires destroyed thousands of hectares of valuable timber.

SUBJECT: forest fires   OBJECT: timber

PASSIVE: Thousands of hectares of valuable timber were destroyed by forest fires.

1. The geologist found volcanic glass from an eruption 2000 years ago.
2. The sudden blizzard stranded people in their cars along the highway.
3. Meteorologists predict a hurricane in the Caribbean next week.
4. The weather forecaster goes to the station twice a day.
5. The tornado destroyed the town.
6. The avalanche occurred on Whistler Mountain.
7. The avalanche buried three skiers alive.
8. There will be many monsoons in Japan during the rainy season.
9. The tornado picked up the car and deposited it in a tree.
10. The flood caused millions of dollars in damages.

2. Use

The passive voice is used when it is not important to acknowledge the doer of the action, when the doer of the action is obvious, or when we simply don't know who did the action. In these cases we want to emphasize the result of the action or the action itself.

EXAMPLE: Only five survivors have been identified so far.

In this example, we do not care who actually made the identification, so there is no "by" phrase.

Exercise B

Use the following words to create passive sentences. Use the "by" phrase if it is important to know who or what was responsible for the action.

EXAMPLE: floodwaters / town / flood
The town was completely flooded.

In this sentence it is obvious that the town was flooded by floodwaters so there is no need to state the obvious in a "by" phrase.

EXAMPLE: suspect / people / several tenants / kill / blast

People suspect that several tenants were killed in the blast.
OR
Several tenants were killed in the blast.

When the subject of the active sentence is "people," it is often omitted in the passive voice.

1. village / bury / volcanic ash
2. survivors / rescue / passing ship / lifeboats
3. snow / travellers / snowed-in
4. burn / fire / forest
5. trap / rubble / earthquake / people
6. operate / rescue equipment / trained specialist
7. find / wreckage / passing plane
8. town / tornado / destroy
9. 3 a.m. / strike / island / tidal wave
10. announce / prime minister / disaster relief plan

3. Functions

In addition to describing actions, the passive voice has the following functions.

Functions of the Passive Voice

Function	Example
To describe characteristics	Two-thirds of the earth is covered by water.
To describe conditions or processes	Volcanic glass is formed from cooled lava.
To describe locations	The volcano is located just 10 kilometres from here.
To describe a relationship	Scientists are fascinated by the destructive forces of nature.
To describe reason or purpose	A seismograph is used to measure the severity of an earthquake.
To define	A tidal wave is also known as a tsunami.

The preceding uses are seldom formed with a "by" phrase as they are not describing an activity. They are often used with prepositions such as *to, with, in, for, from,* and *by* ("by" in this case has a different meaning than to describe the agent of the action).

Grammar In Use

1. It is common to find the passive voice used extensively in newspaper reports. Reporters generally take "poetic licence" with the language, however, and leave out the *be* form of the verb.

   Look at the following newspaper headlines and expand them. Then rewrite them in the active voice.

   EXAMPLE: Hundreds feared dead as volcano buries village

   EXPANDED HEADLINE: Hundreds of people are feared dead as volcanic eruption buries village

ACTIVE VOICE: We fear that hundreds of people are dead due to a volcanic eruption that buried the village.

a) Island "totally destroyed" by hurricane
b) 180 000 left homeless in southern Florida
c) Death toll expected to top 5000
d) Death toll rises as boats tossed onto sidewalks
e) Hundreds swept to their deaths as tsunami hits coast

2. Now look back at the reading on page 3 and write newspaper headlines for the natural disasters mentioned.

Writing

1. Write a newspaper article describing the most recent natural disaster that you are familiar with. Be sure to include at least three examples of passive voice.

2. Working in teams of three or four, design the ideal natural disaster shelter and write a short journal article entitled "How To Build Your Personal Disaster Shelter."

Speaking

Your younger brother or sister is home alone when a warning of a natural disaster occurs. Identify the disaster and give your sibling explicit instructions over the phone about what he or she should do to survive.

Listening 1

T1.a

Before You Listen

In teams of four or five, share the following information.

1. "My father always knows when it is going to rain because his arthritis starts to really bother him." What are some common folk ways you have identified to predict the weather in North America?

2. What are some of the folk ways that people in your native country use to predict the weather?

Focused Listening

You will hear different individuals telling you how they predict certain weather patterns. Listen for the answers to these questions.

1. What does it mean if the salt stays dry on the onion?

2. Which way does a swan usually fly?

3. What colour of the sky indicates danger?

4. What is the significance of a groundhog seeing its shadow?

5. How do pets indicate an earthquake is about to happen?

One Step Beyond

Often, the chance of surviving a natural disaster is greatly increased if there is a previously established disaster emergency plan. Work in small teams and select a type of disaster that could potentially happen in your area. Your team is responsible for developing the disaster emergency plan for the school. Consider the following:

- supplies to have on hand
- where to go
- who will lead
- what to do during and after the disaster

Make a five-minute presentation to your class outlining your plan. Use visual aids such as a flow chart to make your plan clear.

Vocabulary 2

Proverbs passed down from generation to generation sometimes focus on ways to predict the weather. Proverbs are easy to remember because they are catchy phrases that sometimes rhyme. Working with a partner, complete the following proverbs and cross-word puzzle. Each missing word rhymes with the last word of the previous line.

When the wind is in the east,

'Tis neither good for man nor _____, *(1 Across)*

When the wind is in the north,

The skillful fisher goes not _____; *(2 Across)*

When the wind is in the south,

It blows the bait in the fishes' _____; *(3 Down)*

When the wind is in the west,

Then 'tis at the very _____ . *(1 Down)*

When the dew is on the grass,

Rain will never come to _____. *(3 Across)*

Red sky at night,

Sailors _____. *(4 Down)*

Red sky in morning,

Sailors take _____. *(2 Down)*

Speaking

Your team is responsible for presenting the local weather forecast on the news tonight. Watch a few newscasts to identify the types of broadcasts forecasters typically present and listen for common phrases used to describe the weather. Your forecast should be two to three minutes long and present weather occurring in several regions. Come up with a headline for each story you present.

Reading 2

Native peoples in North America have always respected nature. Their strong beliefs and their understanding of the power of nature are evident in their myths – the stories that explain natural occurrences.

Before You Read

In teams of four or five, discuss the following.

1. Who are the native people of your original country?

2. What are the distinct features of this native culture?

3. Is this culture still strong or has it been overshadowed by other more dominant cultures?

4. You will read one of three myths by different native peoples. The first myth tells how weather is controlled, the second describes how the Earth was formed, and the third describes the origin of corn. Are you familiar with any similar myths or views from the native people of your original country? Describe them.

Jigsaw Reading

Divide into three teams. Each team will read one myth and complete the questions that follow. Then form a new team with one person from each of the other groups and tell your teammates about the passage you read. Like the native peoples who passed on their myths and history orally, you will be passing on your new knowledge orally without looking at the text.

"The Storyteller: The Artist and His Grandfather" by Ojibway artist Norval Morrisseau

Ga-oh, Spirit of the Winds

Though of giant proportions, Ga-oh, who governs the winds, is confined in the broad north sky. Were Ga-oh free, he would tear the heavens into fragments.

In the ages of his solitary confinement, he does ⁵ not forget his strength, and punishes the winds to subjection when they suddenly rear for flight.

At the entrance of his abode and reined to his hands are four watchers: the Bear (north wind), Panther (west wind), Moose (east wind), and Fawn (south wind). ¹⁰ When Ga-oh unbinds Bear, it leads its hurricane winter winds to Earth; when he loosens Panther, its stealthy west winds creep down and follow Earth with their snarling blasts; when Moose is released, its east wind meets the Sun and its misty breath floats ¹⁵ over the Sun's path blinding it with rains; and when Ga-oh unlocks his reins from Fawn, its soothing south winds whisper to Earth and she summons her Spring, who comes planting the seeds for the summer sunglow.

²⁰ Though in his subjugation of the winds it is Ga-oh's duty to pacify them, frequently they are influenced by his varying moods. When Ga-oh is contented and happy, gentle and invigorating breezes fan Earth; when he is irritated by his confinement and restless, ²⁵ strong winds agitate the waters and bend the forest trees; and when, frenzied to mighty throes, Ga-oh becomes vehement, ugly blasts go forth, uprooting trees, dashing the streams into leaping furies, lifting the sea waters to mountainous waves, and devastating ³⁰ the Earth.

Notwithstanding these outbursts, Ga-oh is faithful in disciplining the winds to their proper seasons, and guarding Earth from the rage of the elements.

When the north wind blows strong, the Iroquois ³⁵ say, "The Bear is prowling the sky;" if the west wind is violent, "The Panther is whining." When the east wind chills with its rain, "The Moose is spreading his breath;" and when the south wind wafts soft breezes, "The Fawn is returning to its Doe."

(2)   *confined:* kept somewhere by force

(6)   *subjection:* under someone's or something's control

(7)   *abode:* home or shelter

(7)   *reined:* tied for the purpose of control

(12)   *stealthy:* careful and quiet

(26)   *frenzied:* uncontrolled or extremely excited behaviour

(27)   *vehement:* expressing strong feelings

Comprehension Check

1. Which wind is responsible for the beautiful weather of spring and summer?

2. Who causes hurricanes and tidal waves when angry?

3. Which animal is associated with the east wind?

4. What would happen if Ga-oh were to get loose?

5. Summarize the myth in five or six sentences so that you can retell it to others.

One Step Beyond

Discuss the relationship between human, beast, and nature in this myth. How does the myth support or refute the concept of humans controlling nature?

How the World Was Made

The Earth is a great island floating in a sea of water, and suspended at each of the four cardinal points by a cord hanging down from the sky vault, which is of solid rock. When the world grows old and worn out,
5 the people will die and the cords will break and let the Earth sink down into the ocean, and all will be water again. The Indians are afraid of this.

When all was water, the animals were above in Gălûñ'lătĭ, beyond the arch; but it was very much
10 crowded, and they were wanting more room. They wondered what was below the water, and at last Dâyuni'sĭ, "Beaver's Grandchild," the little Waterbeetle, offered to go and see if it could learn. It darted in every direction over the surface of the
15 water, but could find no firm place to rest. Then it dived to the bottom and came up with some soft mud, which began to grow and spread on every side until it became the island which we call Earth. It was afterward fastened to the sky with four cords, but no
20 one remembers who did this.

At first the Earth was flat and very soft and wet. The animals were anxious to get down, and sent out different birds to see if it was yet dry, but they found no place to alight and came back to Gălûñ'lătĭ. At last
25 it seemed to be time, and they sent out the Buzzard and told him to go and make ready for them. This was the Great Buzzard, the father of all the buzzards we see now. He flew all over the Earth, low down near the ground, and it was still soft. When he
30 reached the Cherokee country, he was very tired, and his wings began to flap and strike the ground, and wherever they struck the Earth there was a valley, and where they turned up again there was a mountain. When the animals above saw this, they were afraid
35 that the whole world would be mountains, so they called him back, but the Cherokee country remains full of mountains to this day.

(2) *cardinal:* main

(3) *vault:* roof supported by arches

(9) *arch:* curved columns that join at a point to form an opening or support for a roof

(24) *alight:* to land on something

Comprehension Check

1. Where did everyone and everything live before the Earth was formed?

2. Which animal was responsible for forming the Earth?

3. How were the valleys formed in Cherokee country?

4. How will the world end?

5. Summarize the myth in five or six sentences so that you can retell it to others.

One Step Beyond

What similarities can you find between this myth and other world creation stories?

The Story of Corn

Some years ago the Ottawa inhabited the Manatoline Islands. However they were driven out by their enemies and left the islands uninhabited except for a [shaman] named Masswaweinini who remained to guard the
5 beautiful islands.

One morning Masswaweinini rose early and walked a long distance through the woods, hunting for game. He began to walk across a wide prairie, when a tiny man with red feathers in his hair suddenly appeared and
10 said "Good morning, Masswaweinini. You are a very strong man, are you not?"

"Yes," replied Masswaweinini, "I am as strong as any man, but no stronger."

The tiny man then pulled out his tobacco-pouch and
15 pipe.

"Come and smoke with me," he said, "and then we must have a wrestling match. If you can throw me, you must say, 'I have thrown Wagemena.'"

So they smoked together, but when the little man
20 was ready to wrestle, Masswaweinini did not like to do it, for he was afraid he might hurt the tiny fellow. But the other insisted, and so they began to wrestle. The little man was very strong and quick, and Masswaweinini felt himself growing weaker every
25 moment. But at last he succeeded in tripping the man with the red feathers, and he fell. Then Masswaweinini said, "I have thrown you, Wagemena." At once the little man vanished, and in his place lay an ear of corn, with a red tassel where the feathers had been. As he stood
30 staring at it the corn spoke. "Pick me up," it said, "and

pull off my outer covering. Then take off my kernels and scatter them over the ground. Break my cob into three parts and throw them near the trees. Depart, but come back after one moon, and see what has
35 happened."

Masswaweinini did exactly as the corn had told him, and went away. When he came back he was surprised to find green blades of corn coming through the ground where the kernels had been scattered. And nearby
40 pumpkin vines were growing where the cobs of corn had been thown.

One day, when summer was nearly over, he paddled his canoe around the island until he came near the wrestling ground. He stepped ashore and to his great
45 astonishment, he found the corn in full ear. He pulled some ripened ears of corn. Then a voice spoke to him from the corn. "You have conquered me Masswaweinini," it said. "If you had not done so, you would have been killed yourself. But your strength
50 made you win the victory, and now you shall always have my body for food. It will be nourishment for you and your tribe."

Thus the Ottawa were given the gift of maize; and to this day their descendants are noted for the care that
55 they take of their immense fields of corn.

(29) *tassel:* the hairlike silky threads at the end of a corn cob

(32) *cob:* the inside core of an ear of corn

(53) *maize:* another word for corn

Comprehension Check

1. Who did Masswaweinini meet on the prairie?
2. What was the origin of the corn?
3. How long did it take for the corn to grow?
4. Summarize the myth in five or six sentences so that you can retell it to others.

One Step Beyond

1. Who do you think the tiny man was? What does he represent?
2. In what other cultures that you know of does corn play an important role?
3. How do native peoples show their respect for nature?

Writing

Write a short legend told in your native country which explains climatic changes. If you do not know a weather legend, then write a local legend explaining a physical landform or an important event. When you have finished, read your legend to the class to determine if different cultures have similar legends.

Grammar Focus 2

PASSIVE VERB TENSES

When forming the passive voice, remember that the verb *be* demonstrates the tense of the sentence.

Tense	Active Voice	Passive Voice be + past participle
Simple present	finds	*is* found
Present continuous	is finding	*is being* found
Simple past	found	*was* found
Past continuous	was finding	*was being* found
Present perfect	has found	*has been* found
Past perfect	had found	*had been* found
Future	will find	*will be* found
Conditional	would find	*would be* found
Perfect conditional	would have found	*would have been* found
Present infinitive	to find	*to be* found
Perfect infinitive	to have found	*to have been* found
Present participle	finding	*being* found
Perfect participle	having found	*having been* found
Auxiliary + infinitive	must find	*must be* found

It is quite rare to find the perfect continuous forms in the passive.

Intransitive verbs never take an object. The following verbs cannot be used in the passive voice.

agree	cry	happen
rain	stay	arrive
exist	live	rise
walk	come	go
occur	sleep	

Exercise A

Identify the tense of the verbs in the following passive sentences.

1. The corn was nurtured by the women.

2. The winds are being confined by Ga-oh.

3. Native myths are passed down orally.

4. Native history would not have been written down thousands of years ago.

5. Appreciation of native culture is being encouraged through educational programs.

Exercise B

Read the following passage identifying the sentences in passive voice and the tense of the passive verbs. Then rewrite the passage using only active voice.

Global warming could have catastrophic effects for our planet. The impending doom of planet Earth due to our continued abuses has been predicted by scientists over the last decade. Heat from the sun is being trapped by gases such as carbon dioxide causing a gradual rise in world temperatures. Carbon dioxide is formed by burning fossil fuels which people find difficult to do without. Future generations will be affected by our refusal to radically change how we live. Scientists predict that if current patterns continue, low-lying coastal land will be submerged by rising sea levels. Warmer winters and increased hot spells will be experienced by people all over the world. Increased flooding and droughts will occur in many areas. Temperature and rainfall patterns will be shifted in unpredictable ways by global warming. Scientists believe that it is virtually impossible for nations to work cooperatively to save our planet and that we should in fact be spending our research dollars on strategies to deal with the unavoidable consequences of global warming.

Tip

The passive voice is more common in written than in spoken English. It is very common in academic or technical writing such as journal articles and scientific reports because it appears to be more objective. The writer is able to eliminate any personal viewpoint or bias associated with the active voice.

A. I recorded the wind velocity each half hour.

B. The wind velocity was recorded each half hour.

Sentence B is far more objective than sentence A. It is regarded as more formal and, therefore, is the preferred style for academic reporting.

Grammar In Use

Write a short article describing your observations about one of the following situations. Make your article as objective as possible.

a) The effects of global warming in your country

b) The economic reasons global warming will not realistically be addressed by every country

c) The impact of clear-cut logging on the ecosystem

d) The impact of technological advances on our environment

Scientist David Suzuki (left) and writer Farley Mowat are outspoken environmentalists.

Listening 2

T1.b

You will hear excerpts from an interview between Farley Mowat and David Suzuki. Farley Mowat is a Canadian writer known for his outspoken views on our treatment of nature and the environment. David Suzuki is a world-famous Canadian scientist who crusades to save the environment.

Before You Listen

In teams of four or five, discuss the following questions.

1. In an interview with *Newsweek*, Farley Mowat is quoted as saying "Modern man is such an arrogant cement head to believe that he can take without paying." What do you think he means by this?

2. David Suzuki believes that most scientists are incapable of looking at the "big picture" of nature and focus only on micro aspects. Why might this be a problem?

3. Give examples of ways in which modern humans try to conquer nature and ways in which we try to co-exist peacefully with it.

Comprehension Check

1. What does Farley Mowat mean when he says that we can only know nature by becoming part of it?

2. According to David Suzuki, what is modern human's relationship with nature? Give an example.

3. According to David Suzuki, what have been the two most significant changes in our relationship with nature since the beginning of human existence? Why do these changes pose a serious danger?

One Step Beyond

1. What solutions could you offer David Suzuki for the problems he poses?

2. What environmental and population management policies are there in your country?

3. Many of these issues are not just local, they are global. How can we work together to form solutions?

Unit Reflection

Nature images can be found in all aspects of our lives. Phrases such as "the calm before the storm" are often used to describe general truths, human emotions, and so on. Other sayings include:

"The sun always rises."

"Behind every cloud is a silver lining."

What other phrases related to nature do you commonly hear and how do these sayings apply to our everyday lives?

Unit 2

Strange But True

DISCUSSION

1. Who is Albert Einstein?

2. Read the quote below. In your own words, describe what Einstein thinks about "the mysterious."

3. What are some mysterious phenomena and how have people tried to explain them in various cultures?

The most beautiful experience we can have is the mysterious. It is the fundamental emotion which stands at the cradle of true art and true science. Whoever does not know it and can no longer wonder, no longer marvel, is as good as dead, and his eyes are dimmed.

Albert Einstein

Vocabulary 1

a. astrology	f. clairvoyance	j. levitation	n. seance
b. medium	g. numerology	k. omen	o. telepathy
c. premonition	h. psychic	l. reincarnation	p. shaman
d. subconscious	i. curse	m. poltergeist	q. voodoo
e. psychokinesis			

Match the words to the meanings below. Use a dictionary to help you.

1. ☐ A level of thoughts and memories just below the surface of the conscious mind.

2. ☐ A sign that heralds either good or bad luck to the one who sees it.

3. ☐ A feeling, dream, or vision about something which will happen in the future.

4. ☐ The ability to move objects through mind power.

5. ☐ Rising off the ground in defiance of gravity.

6. ☐ The belief that numbers have meaning and can be used to read a person's character and future.

7. ☐ A spiritualist cult based in Haiti; called Hoodoo in parts of America.

8. ☐ The study of how the planets influence the character and future of people.

9. ☐ A meeting led by a medium in which spirits of the dead are contacted.

10. ☐ The power to see clearly in the mind images or events that are happening out of sight or in the future.

11. ☐ Someone who, for some reason, can be used as a go-between or a "telephone line" between this world and the "next."

12. ☐ A "noisy ghost" often associated with children and thought to be either a manifestation of psychokinesis (PK) or a troublesome spirit.

13. ☐ The rebirth of the soul, usually as another person, but sometimes as an animal or a demon.

14. ☐ Spiritual leader of tribal communities, including North American Native communities, who can communicate with the spirit world, cure illnesses, etc.

15. ☐ An appeal to a supernatural power for harm to come to a person or group of people. Also called malediction or hex.

16. ☐ The ability to communicate by thought alone.

17. ☐ Sensitivity to forces outside the natural laws of science, or someone with this sensitivity.

The absence of evidence is not the evidence of absence.

Terence Dickinson

Discussion

All of the phenomena on the previous page can be considered supernatural. In teams, discuss the differences and similarities in meaning among the following terms: *supernatural*, *mysterious*, and *mystical*. Write a definition for each term. Then compare your definitions with those of other teams.

You will hear a true account of a paranormal experience one young Canadian had during the Second World War. The story is taken from John Robert Colombo's book *Mysterious Encounters*, a collection of reported supernatural experiences in Canada.

Before You Listen

In small groups, discuss these questions and share your experiences.

1. What do you think is the significance of dreams? Do you think dreams have any connection with spirituality?

2. Have you ever had recurring dreams or a powerful dream that left a lasting impression? How might you interpret these dreams?

3. Do you know of anyone who had a dream that later came true? Describe the dream.

Focused Listening

Harry Stevens, a native of Cameron, Ontario, had a very strange experience during the Second World War. While stationed in Europe, he came upon a house which he had dreamed about as a child in Canada. Listen to the account and list all of the facts supporting the idea that this house was the house of Harry's dreams.

For Discussion

1. Harry Stevens asks: "Had I lived in that house in some previous life, before being reincarnated to a Canadian life?" What evidence is there that makes him consider this alternative?

2. He also wonders whether some mysterious soul from the past had been put to rest by his finding that house. What does Harry say at the end of his story that suggests this might be true?

One Step Beyond

What possible explanations can you offer for this occurrence?

Before You Read

Many people have claimed to have had near-death experiences in which they glimpse the "next" world. Descriptions of these experiences are surprisingly similar. In teams, share what you have heard or read about such claims. What common elements can you find in these descriptions?

Applying Meaning Through Context

You will read an account of a near-death experience from the journals of the famous psychiatrist Carl Gustav Jung. The account describes the experience of one of Jung's patients. Some of the sentences have been left out. Read the passage and insert the sentences listed on the next page where you think they fit.

Between Two Worlds

A woman patient, whose reliability and truthfulness I have no reason to doubt, told me that her first birth was very difficult. After thirty hours of fruitless labour the doctor considered that a forceps delivery was
5 indicated. This was carried out under light narcosis. She was badly torn and suffered great loss of blood. When the doctor, her mother, and her husband had gone, and everything was cleared up, the nurse wanted to eat, and the patient saw her turn around at the
10 door and ask, "Do you want anything before I go to supper?" [1._____] She had the feeling that she was sinking through the bed into a bottomless void. She saw the nurse hurry to the bedside and seize her hand in order to take her pulse. From the
15 way she moved her fingers to and fro the patient thought it must have been almost imperceptible. Yet she herself felt quite all right, and was slightly amused at the nurse's alarm. [2._____] That was the last she could remember for a long time.
20 The next thing she was aware of was that, without feeling her body and its position, she was looking down from a point in the ceiling and could see everything going on in the room below her: she saw

25 herself lying in the bed, deadly pale, with closed eyes. Beside her stood the nurse. The doctor paced up and down the room excitedly, and it seemed to her that he had lost his head and didn't know what to do. Her relatives crowded to the door. Her mother and her husband came in and looked at her with fright-
30 ened faces. She told herself it was too stupid of them to think she was going to die, for she would certainly come round again.

All this time she knew that behind her was a glorious, park-like landscape shining in the brightest
35 colours, and in particular an emerald green meadow with short grass, which sloped gently upwards beyond a wrought-iron gate leading into the park. It was spring, and little gay flowers such as she had never seen before were scattered about in the grass.
40 The whole demesne sparkled in the sunlight, and all the colours were of an indescribable splendour. The sloping meadow was flanked on both sides by dark green trees. [3._____] "I knew that this was the entrance to another world, and that if I
45 turned round to gaze at the picture directly, I should feel tempted to go in at the gate, and thus step out of life." She did not actually see this landscape, as her

Sentences to be inserted in reading:

a) It gave her the impression of a clearing in the forest, never yet trodden by the foot of man.

b) The nurse energetically denied this criticism in the belief that the patient had been completely unconscious at the time and could therefore have known nothing of the scene.

c) She was not in the least frightened.

d) That was why she found the agitation of the doctor and the distress of her relatives stupid and out of place.

e) She tried to answer, but couldn't.

Comprehension Check

Are the following statements true (T) or false (F)?

1. ☐ The patient died.

2. ☐ The woman had been unconscious for about half an hour.

3. ☐ The patient thought her relatives were stupid.

4. ☐ The patient delivered her baby in spring.

5. ☐ The woman felt tempted to gaze at a picture on the wall.

6. ☐ The woman was in labour for more than twenty hours.

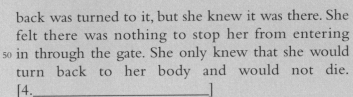

back was turned to it, but she knew it was there. She felt there was nothing to stop her from entering
50 in through the gate. She only knew that she would turn back to her body and would not die. [4._____]

The next thing that happened was that she awoke from her coma and saw the nurse bending over her
55 in bed. She was told that she had been unconscious for about half an hour. The next day, some fifteen hours later, when she felt a little stronger, she made a remark to the nurse about the incompetent and "hysterical" behaviour of the doctor during her coma.
60 [5._____] Only when she described in full detail what had happened during the coma was the nurse obliged to admit that the patient had perceived the events exactly as they happened in reality.
65 One might conjecture that this was simply a psychogenic twilight state in which a split-off part of consciousness still continued to function. The patient, however, had never been hysterical and had suffered a genuine heart collapse. She really was in a
70 coma and ought to have had a complete psychic black-out and been altogether incapable of clear observation and sound judgement.

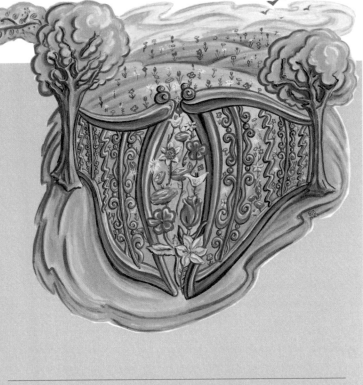

(5) *narcosis*: a sleeping drug

(16) *imperceptible*: unnoticeable

(40) *demesne*: scene

(42) *flanked*: bordered

(54) *coma*: state of unconsciousness

(65) *conjecture*: guess

Sentence Meanings

Find the sentences in the reading that mean the same as the sentences below.

1. The woman had been in labour for a long time without results. The doctor decided to intervene.

2. The patient felt as though she were falling.

3. The patient concluded from the nurse's reaction that her pulse was barely noticeable.

4. The woman had an out-of-body experience and could see everything happening in the room.

5. The landscape she saw was bright and the colours were extremely beautiful.

6. Confident that the patient was unaware of what had happened, the nurse covered up for the doctor's inappropriate behaviour by claiming it didn't happen.

Discuss the Reading

1. Why did Jung believe the patient's version of the experience?

2. Why was the patient not afraid?

3. The woman describes the park-like landscape as "a clearing in the forest, never yet trodden by the foot of man." What do you think she means by this?

One Step Beyond

1. What about this reading makes it believable?

2. What significance does the "gate" have in the woman's vision?

3. What makes the description of the landscape so appealing?

Speaking

The account you have just read was told by C.G. Jung, the patient's psychiatrist. However, several people were present at this incident: the patient, the nurse, the husband, the patient's mother, and the physician. Work in teams of three or four. Each of you should choose one of these characters and retell the story to your team from the perspective of that character. Speak in the first person, "I". Let your teammates judge how well you were able to focus on that character's perspective of the story.

The sceptic does not mean the one who doubts, but the one who inquires and searches, as opposed to the one who asserts and supposes he has found.

Miguel De Unamuno, from "My Religion," 1924

There is no credible evidence that life survives the death of the body.

Humanist Manifesto II

Writing

Write a paragraph about an unusual or unexplained incident you have experienced or seen in a movie or on television.

People have experienced strange and inexplicable phenomena for centuries.

Grammar Focus 1

REPORTED SPEECH – STATEMENTS

A. Use

There are two ways of relating what a person says:

1. Using the exact words of the speaker (quoted or direct speech)

EXAMPLE: Harry Stevens said, "The dream came back so many times that it seemed real to me at the time."

The exact words of the speaker are placed between quotation marks preceded by a comma (,"...").

2. Relaying the message of the speaker without using the speaker's exact words (reported or indirect speech)

EXAMPLE: Harry Stevens said (that) the dream had come back so many times that it had seemed real to him at the time.

In this case, we are accurately relaying what Harry Stevens said, but we are not using his exact words.

Vocabulary 2

Prefixes and Meaning

Some English words have groups of letters attached at the beginning that add meaning. These groups of letters are called prefixes.

1. Discuss the meaning of the following words. Look in a dictionary if necessary. Then, explain the meaning of the underlined prefixes.

<u>pre</u>monition	<u>super</u>natural	<u>tele</u>pathy
<u>sub</u>conscious	<u>syn</u>chronicity	
<u>para</u>normal		

2. Based on your knowledge of the prefixes, explain the meaning of the following words.

   a) *pre*cognition
      *pre*requisite

   b) *super*impose
      *super*ficial

   c) *syn*thesize
      *syn*onymous

   d) *tele*cast
      *tele*photo

   e) *sub*topic
      *sub*ordinate

   f) *para*psychology
      *para*phrase

3. In teams, find two more examples for each prefix and write these words on a paper. Exchange your paper with another team. Have that team deduce the meaning of your words and write a sentence for each one. Finally, collect your words again and check that the sentences are correct and the meanings of the words have been understood.

- In reported speech we use a reporting verb, such as *say*, to introduce the "meaning" of the original speaker's remarks. (For a list of reporting verbs, see the Appendix on page 159.)

- The word *that* is optional after the reporting verbs *say* or *tell*, but should be kept after other reporting verbs such as *explain, point out, announce,* etc.

- Reported speech has no quotation marks or question marks.

B. Structure

When we convert quoted speech into reported speech, we often change the following to give an accurate account of what the original speaker said:

1. verb tenses
2. pronouns and possessive adjectives
3. expressions of time and place

These elements change because the quoted speech is being expressed from the reporter's, rather than the original speaker's, point of view.

1. Changes in Verb Tense

Reporting Verb – Present Tense: *She says that ... He tells me that ... etc.*

Reporting verbs in the present tense are commonly used when:

a) reporting a conversation that is still going on
b) reading a letter and reporting what it says
c) reading instructions and reporting them
d) reporting a statement about something someone does very often, e.g., Maria says she reads her horoscope every day.

When the reporting verb is in a present, present perfect, or future tense, we often report the quoted speech without any change in tense.

EXAMPLE: ROBERT (on the telephone to Yvonne):
   Hi Yvonne. What are you doing?
   YVONNE (on the telephone to Robert):
   I'm reading my horoscope.
   ROBERT (to Julio standing beside him):
   Yvonne says she*'s reading* her horoscope.

Grammar Focus 1

Changes in Verb Tenses: Quoted to Reported Speech

Quoted Speech	Reported Speech
Simple present	*Simple past*
"I *don't* believe in astrology," he explained.	He explained (that) he *didn't* believe in astrology.
Present continuous	*Past continuous*
"I*'m reading* a book about reincarnation," she said.	She said (that) she *was reading* a book about reincarnation.
Present perfect	*Past perfect*
"I *have* never *participated* in a seance,"he exclaimed.	He said (that) he *had* never *participated* in a seance.
Present perfect continuous	*Past perfect continuous*
She said, "I*'ve been studying* psychic phenomena for years."	She said she *had been studying* psychic phenomena for years.
Simple past	*Past perfect*
"I *had* a premonition," he said.	He said he *had had* a premonition.
Future	*Conditional*
The psychic said, "You *will marry* a rich widow."	The psychic said he *would marry* a rich widow.
Future continuous	*Conditional continuous*
"I *will be attending* a palm reading next week," she said.	She said she *would be attending* a palm reading next week.

When the reporting verb is in the past tense but the statement refers to a general fact that is still true, the reported speech doesn't necessarily require a change in tense. The first example in the chart could be reported simply as "He explained that he *doesn't* believe in astrology."

Exercise A

Convert the quoted speech into reported speech changing the tenses as required.

1. The psychiatrist said, "The patient's dream is quite revealing."

2. The counsellor said, "The patient has experimented with psychokinetic powers."

3. The psychiatrist said, "The patient has been having premonitions."

4. The counsellor said, "The patient won't remember the strange event."

5. The psychiatrist said, "Mrs. Acker will never forget the experience."

2. Changes in Pronouns and Possessive Adjectives

Pronouns may have to be changed to reflect accurately the meaning of the quoted speech.

EXAMPLES: She said, *"I've* just seen a ghost."
She said that *she* had just seen a ghost.

He said, "I will tell *your* future."
He said he would tell *my* future.

Sometimes we have to use a noun in place of a pronoun to clarify the meaning of the reported speech.

EXAMPLE: Carlos said, "*He* walked right through the wall."
Carlos said that *the apparition* had walked right through the wall.

The apparition (in this case a male figure) is used in place of the pronoun *he*, otherwise the sentence may imply that Carlos himself had walked through the wall.

Exercise B

Change the quoted speech to reported speech.

1. The young woman said, "I floated out of my body and looked down on the scene below me."

2. The young man said, "I floated out of my body and looked down on the scene below me."

3. The young man said to me, "I will show you the place where I saw the beast."

4. The young woman said to us, "I will show you the place where I saw the beast."

5. The young children said to their grandfather, "We will show you the place where we saw the beast."

3. a) Changes in Time Expressions

Expressions of time may have to be changed to reflect accurately the meaning of the quoted speech.

Let logic guide you in determining what changes need to be made.

EXAMPLE: On Monday Sheila says to Amrita, "I'm seeing a psychic the day after tomorrow."
If Amrita reports this on Tuesday, she will

Changes in Time Expressions

Quoted Speech	Reported Speech
today	that day
yesterday	the day before
the day before yesterday	two days before
tomorrow	the next day/the following day
next week/year, etc.	the following week/year, etc.
last week/year, etc.	the previous week/year, etc.
a year (etc.) ago	a year before/the previous year

probably say: "Sheila said she was seeing a psychic tomorrow."
If Amrita reports this on Wednesday, she will probably say: "Sheila said she was seeing a psychic today."

Exercise C

Look at the quoted speech below. Then report the speech from the different time perspectives given. In your answers, include the time when Madame Girard made the announcement.

QUOTED SPEECH: On Wednesday morning Madame Girard announces to her class:

"Next week, we will begin our study of the paranormal."

1. On Wednesday afternoon, Jocelyn reports to a classmate who was absent in the morning: This morning Madame Girard told us that...(what? when?)

2. On Thursday, Jocelyn reports to a classmate who was absent: _____

3. On Monday, Jocelyn reports to a classmate who has been absent for a few days: _____

4. One week later on Thursday, Jocelyn reports to a classmate who was absent all week:_____

Grammar Focus 1

3. b) Changes in Place Expressions

Here can become *there* but only when it is clear what place is meant.

EXAMPLE: Standing in the secret room, Harry Stevens said, "I hid all my valuable toys in *here*."
Harry said that he had hid all his valuable toys in *there*. (meaning the secret room)

Often *here* needs to be replaced by a phrase that more clearly defines the place.

EXAMPLE: He said, "I hid all my valuable toys in *here*."
He said that he had hid all his valuable toys *in the secret room*.

Tip

The key to making changes in reported speech is to use logic. Let your logic guide you more than the rules. The purpose is to make the meaning as clear as possible.

Exercise D

What did the original speaker say? Change the reported speech to quoted speech.

1. He said that he didn't understand what had just happened there.

2. The little boy said that he had seen soldiers marching in battle.

3. The doctor insisted he didn't believe in the paranormal.

4. The woman informed the police that her son had been captured by aliens.

Grammar In Use

Divide the class into two teams. Have one student from any team relate a personal encounter with the supernatural to the class. (You may prefer to relate an encounter seen on a television program or experienced by someone else). When the story is finished, students will report what was said. Alternating between teams, each student, in turn, must report one statement made by the speaker.

Speaking

A Chain Ghost Story

In North America, young and old alike enjoy camping in the outdoors. One favourite activity is telling ghost stories around the campfire at night. Imagine that you are camping in the wilderness with four or five friends and it is midnight. Tell a chain ghost story. One of you should begin with these words: "One hot, dark, stormy night last summer a strange occurrence happened in these very woods. A group of campers, just like us, was camping not far from here. One night, after the last camper crept into his tent, an unusual noise was heard coming from over there (point)." Each person in the group then adds to the story in turn. Use your imagination and some of the vocabulary you have learned in this unit as you continue the story.

> *The soul is indestructible... Its activity will continue throughout eternity.*
>
> 18th century German poet Johann Wolfgang von Goethe

Listening 2

You will hear another account from John Robert Colombo's book *Mysterious Encounters*. Dr. T. J. Muckle first related these events during a radio interview. He then wrote a follow-up letter describing his experience. You will hear his account from this letter, in which he describes a mysterious "apparition."

Before You Listen

Work in teams. Share your experiences.

1. Have you personally ever seen an apparition or known of someone who has?

2. Do you believe that apparitions are possible? Why or why not?

Focused Listening

Read the questions below. Then listen to the account and choose the correct answers.

1. This incident took place in the summer of
   a) 1988.
   b) 1976.
   c) 1966.
   d) 1978.

2. Dr. Muckle was _____ when the sighting happened.
   a) sitting on an easy chair in the living room
   b) sitting in a garden chair on the lawn
   c) sitting in an easy chair on the verandah
   d) standing by the front door of his small bungalow

3. The apparition of the cat
   a) looked completely normal but walked about a foot and a half above the floor.
   b) was surrounded by a glow and walked about a foot and a half above the floor.
   c) had a dark aura.
   d) looked ghost-like and floated through the air.

4. Immediately after seeing the apparition, Dr. Muckle
   a) called two of his children to give him a hand to see if they could find any cat anywhere in or near the bungalow.
   b) called his children and his wife to tell them of the experience.
   c) went inside the bungalow to see if by chance it could have been some sort of optical illusion.
   d) got up and tried to follow the apparition.

5. Two and a half hours later,
   a) Dr. Muckle telephoned his neighbour to see if his cat was alright.
   b) Dr. Muckle received a message that his neighbour had called.
   c) Dr. Muckle had a strong feeling that his cat had died.
   d) Dr. Muckle's wife informed him that their cat had died three hours earlier.

For Discussion

1. How did Dr. Muckle feel when he saw the apparition?

2. What did Dr. Muckle do to confirm that he had indeed seen an apparition?

3. Dr. Muckle says, "I immediately wondered whether I would have seen the apparition had the cat died instantly – the implication I trust is obvious." What does he mean by this?

One Step Beyond

Why do you think Dr. Muckle adds at the end that this was the only experience he had had with the paranormal?

Sequencing Events

Immediately after the experience, Dr. Muckle may have written down a few key points to help him remember the sequence of events. The points on the next page are not in the correct order. Put them in the correct order. Then listen to the story again to check your answers.

a) ☐ suddenly, see pet cat walking calmly across room

b) ☐ cat walked across room above floor level and, before reached other wall, disappeared

c) ☐ experience was not frightening

d) ☐ several days after arriving, sitting on bungalow verandah in afternoon, reading book

e) ☐ other than walking above floor level, nothing strange about cat

f) ☐ chair sideways, so could see living room through door from corner of eye

Grammar Focus 2

REPORTED SPEECH – QUESTIONS

As with statements, when we convert quoted questions into reported speech we also change:

1. tense

2. pronouns and possessive adjectives

3. adverbs of time and place

The question form, however, changes to the statement form when reported.

QUOTED: She said, "*Have **you** ever seen an apparition **here**?*"

REPORTED: She asked if *I had* ever seen an apparition ***there.***

The reported form does not need a question mark (?) because it is no longer a question. However, to let the listener know that the original speaker had asked a question, we use the reporting verb *ask*.

- **Changes in Word Order** – The inverted question form *have you ever seen* changes to the statement form *I had ever seen.*

- **Changes in Verb Tense** – The present perfect tense *have you seen* changes to the past perfect tense *I had seen.*

- **Changes in Pronouns and Possessive Adjectives** – The pronoun *you* in *have you ever seen* changes to *I* in *I had ever seen.*

- **Changes in Time and Place Expressions** – The adverb *here* changes to the adverb *there.*

Information Questions

If there is a question word (*who, what, where, when, how*) in the quoted form, it is repeated in the reported form.

QUOTED: "*When did you see this ghost?*" she asked.

REPORTED: She asked *(me) when* I had seen the ghost.

* the verb *ask* can take an indirect object. Other verbs of inquiry don't take an object. For a list of common verbs of inquiry, see the Appendix on page 159.

Writing

1. Write a letter to a friend retelling the account of the apparition as if you had just heard it on the radio. Use reported speech where appropriate.

2. Writing in the round. Working in teams of three or four, write a fictional story about a supernatural experience. Each team member should write a paragraph on a sheet of blank paper that introduces a story from his or her own imagination. Next, exchange paragraphs with the person to the left. Write a second paragraph that continues the story now in front of you. Again, exchange papers with the person to the left. Write a third paragraph that continues the story on the paper, and so on. Once the stories are finished, return them to the original writer. Edit the stories for grammatical errors and then read them to your teammates.

> *The simple imagery of the visions — tunnels, lights, and colours — are probably caused by a discharge of neurons in the eye.*
>
> Psychologist Ronald Siegel

> *As a man casts off his worn-out clothes and takes on other new ones, so does the embodied self cast off its worn-out bodies and enter new ones.*
>
> Hindu holy book *Bhagavad Gita*

Yes/No Questions

If there is no question word in the quoted form, we use *if* or *whether* in the reported form.

QUOTED: She asked, "Did you see a ghost?"
REPORTED: She asked (me) *if* I had seen a ghost.

Exercise A

Change the quoted speech to reported speech.

1. "How did I know there would be a secret room?" Harry asked himself.

2. Turning to the patient, the nurse said, "Do you want anything before I go for supper?"

3. Harry asked himself, "Has some mysterious soul been put to rest by my finding the house?"

4. "Was someone sending me messages through mental telepathy?" wondered Harry.

5. Dr. Muckle wondered, "Why would our neighbours phone us here?"

Grammar In Use

1. Imagine that you are a reporter interviewing Dr. Muckle about his experience with the apparition. Write five questions you would ask him. Then exchange your questions with a partner who will report your questions to the class.

2. Work with a partner. Take turns making one statement about each of the topics below. Then report what your partner said to the class. As a class, note the different perspectives your classmates bring to each topic.

   a) the connection between the supernatural and immortality

   b) the effects of scientific knowledge on the paranormal

   c) control of personal destiny and fate

   d) the relationship between illness and the psyche

Your Astrological Sign

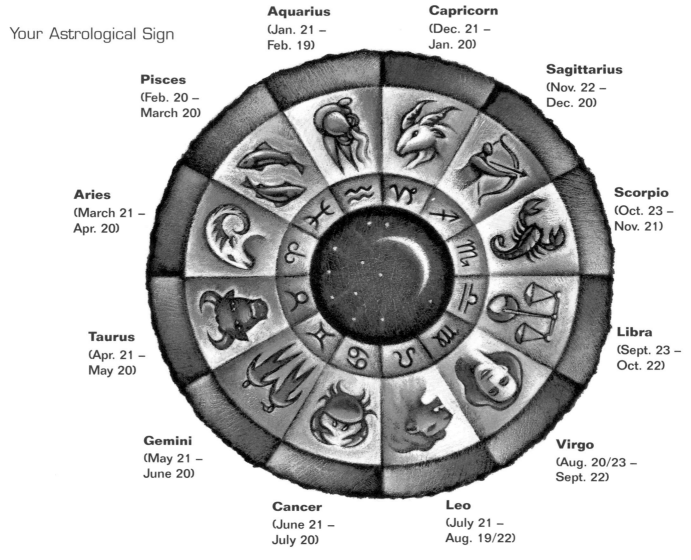

Aquarius (Jan. 21 – Feb. 19)

Capricorn (Dec. 21 – Jan. 20)

Pisces (Feb. 20 – March 20)

Sagittarius (Nov. 22 – Dec. 20)

Aries (March 21 – Apr. 20)

Scorpio (Oct. 23 – Nov. 21)

Taurus (Apr. 21 – May 20)

Libra (Sept. 23 – Oct. 22)

Gemini (May 21 – June 20)

Virgo (Aug. 20/23 – Sept. 22)

Cancer (June 21 – July 20)

Leo (July 21 – Aug. 19/22)

Before You Read

People in all cultures and through time have speculated about the influence the stars have on our lives. In North America, many people read their horoscopes every day (some for fun, some more seriously).

Your birthdate reveals the astrological sign under which you were born – whether you are, for example, an Aries or a Taurus. That tells a believer in astrology quite a lot about you. The signs, and the characteristics said to go with them, are listed according to the astrological year.

Do you have systems for determining a person's character or predicting the future in your native culture? Discuss them with your classmates.

Reading

Work in a team. Read the character descriptions on the next page and then match each one to the correct sign of the zodiac. Look for clues in the descriptions to help you. Then check your answers on page 157.

For Discussion

Think about the characteristics of your own zodiac sign and the sign of others you know. Then discuss whether you agree or disagree with the descriptions.

a) You are an artistic person. You also are a hard worker, and you depend on yourself, not on others. You are practical and patient and you usually are easy to get along with. But you can be as stubborn and determined as a bull. It takes a while for you to get angry, but if someone does anger you, they had better watch out. _____

b) You are a very private person. You tend to be secretive and hard to know, like a crab. You are like a crab in another way. Once you get hold of something, you hang onto it. Your room is filled with things you don't need but won't throw away. _____

c) You love reading and thinking about things. You have opinions about almost everything and you freely express them. Some believe you tend to be too critical; now and then they may be right, but your intentions are as pure as a virgin. _____

d) You tend to balance everything very carefully, like a set of scales, before reaching a decision. You want to be fair and are sympathetic and understanding. As a result, you are slow to make up your mind or take sides in an argument. _____

e) You like being with people and make friends easily. But you tend to say whatever is on your mind. At times you hurt someone's feelings without meaning to. You love sports like archery in which you can compete against yourself or just a few other persons. _____

f) You are for equality. You believe that everyone is special, that there is no such thing as an ordinary person. You also believe that people should do their own thing, as long as they carry their burdens on their own shoulders and no one else suffers. You are intelligent, artistic, generous, and friendly, yet you are unpredictable. Often no one knows what you are going to do next, except that it will be interesting. _____

g) You are lively, adventurous, funny, and full of ideas. You make friends easily, and your friends turn to you to lead them. But you are impatient and stubborn, and not unlike the butting ram, you tend to be irritable when you don't get your way. _____

h) You are a cheerful, lively, changeable person. You are also able to deal with many subjects at one time as if you had a twin. Often you don't finish what you start. You have a tendency to pass up good opportunities. You may readily give up one friend for another, or a job or a sport in which you could be outstanding if only you stuck to it. _____

i) In some ways you are quite a bit like a lion. You are determined and brave and loyal and affectionate. At times you are also bossy, and become angry and roar when someone disagrees with you. _____

j) You are at your best when making and carrying out decisions. But when you let your emotions take over, you can inflict poison like a scorpion. Usually though, you are thoughtful and quiet. _____

k) You are a serious, ambitious person. You don't like fooling around and wasting time. You work at things with patience and care, and are good at meeting challenges and overcoming obstacles. _____

l) You are a gentle, cautious, dreamy person, but you also are moody and changeable. One minute you may be as lively as can be and the next as quiet as can be. You love artistic things, and, just as fish do, you love the water. _____

One Step Beyond

1. Why do you think people want to believe in astrology?

2. What is the significance of associating animals with astrology and human behaviour?

> *Our souls will exist somewhere in another world.*
> 4th century BC Greek philosopher Plato

Unit Reflection

Throughout this unit you have seen quotes about the paranormal or life after death. Read the quotes and discuss which ones support the existence of the paranormal and which ones refute it. What arguments would you give either for or against the existence of the paranormal?

Unit 3

The Road Less Travelled

DISCUSSION

1. What is your definition of a traveller or explorer?
2. What qualities do you think a person must possess to be an explorer?
3. Who are some well-known past and present explorers that you are familiar with?

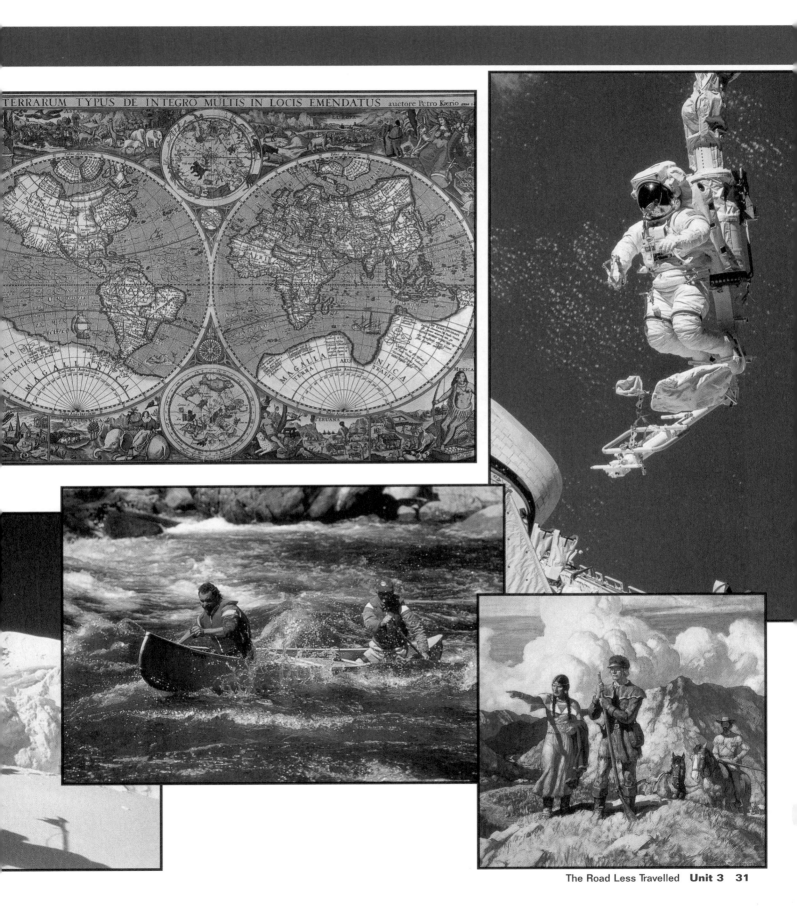

Travel Quiz

WHERE IN THE WORLD IS MARCO?

1. My best friend Marco is travelling around the world. He sends me postcards telling me all about the wonderful sites he's seen and the things he's done, but he never tells me exactly where he is. I always have to guess from his descriptions. Working with a partner, read his postcards to see if you can identify where he's been.

2. Marco had an around-the-world ticket that allowed him to make as many stops as he wanted as long as he continued to travel in the same direction without backtracking. Assume that he started from where you are. Once you have determined from where he has sent the postcards, put them in the order of his destinations. (Check your answers on page 157.)

3. There is some speculation that these were put here by aliens from another planet over 35,000 years ago. Who knows? But ask yourself — how could our ancestors have erected these great stone slabs? They weigh 28-50 tonnes each and are 5-9 metres high.

1. This huge rock rises out of a desert in the centre of the continent. It's 10 km around the base. The challenge is to climb it - it's a lot taller and steeper than it looks - and boy, is it cold at the top. I got to sign my name in a book at the top as a testament to my climb. The Aboriginal people think this rock is sacred.

4. It sure has the SkyDome in Toronto beat. It could hold 48,000 people; that's only 7,000 fewer than the Dome & people would come from all over to watch men test their mettle against wild beasts. What's really unbelievable though is that they used to flood it to hold water battles — an unbelievable feat of ancient engineering.

2. I flew over this in a little nine-seater—what an awesome sight. It's over 322 km long and in places it's over 1,615 m deep. It took millions of years for the river to carve out this masterpiece. What a flight! I was really happy to be back on land.

5. This simple white and green farmhouse is where L.M. Montgomery's cousins lived. When she was writing her book, she used this farmhouse as the location for her heroine, Anne. Over 700,000 people a year visit this tiny island just to see where the fictitious red-haired, pigtailed, lovable child lived.

6. A Mogul emperor built this white marble edifice as a tribute to his wife to keep her memory alive. It took 22 years and over 20,000 people to complete. It looks exactly the same when viewed from any direction. It's a perfect example of Mogul architecture.

7. This is one of the most widely recognized symbols of freedom throughout the world. It was a gift from France to celebrate the friendship and aid that France gave America when it was fighting for its independence from Britain. I climbed right up to the tip of the torch. What a view!

9. This ancient culture thought that the dead would live again so they built these elaborate burial places containing all the riches the dead would need for their new lives — artifacts like gold jewellery and dishes. Immense statues with lions' bodies and human heads stand guard to remind everyone of how great the person buried there was.

10. Can you believe it? This falls drops 979 m. It's the tallest in South America, located in the midst of a thick tropical rain forest. It was actually named after an American pilot who discovered it after making a forced landing in 1937. It makes Niagara Falls seem quite small in comparison.

8. Do you know that this is the one man-made thing that can be seen from the moon? It would take someone hiking day and night for seven weeks to travel its 2,000 km length. It was built in the 5th century B.C. as a defence against wandering tribes.

ADJECTIVE ORDER IN DESCRIPTIONS

1. Determining Adjective Order

To create a clear, detailed picture of what we are describing, we qualify a noun with several descriptive words (adjectives) to evoke an image in the mind of the listener or reader. These adjectives generally follow a specific word order, though there are variations.

EXAMPLE: The *huge, ornate, 18th century marble* palace was a highlight of the tour.

Adjective Order	
Order/Type of Adjective	**Examples**
1. determiner	*three, our*
2. size (except *little*)	*huge, small, tiny*
3. general description (excluding adjectives of personality, emotion, etc.)	*interesting, influential*
4. age and the adjective *little*	*two-year-old, ancient*
5. shape	*round, curvy*
6. colour	*black, opaque*
7. material	*wood, stone*
8. origin	*Canadian, Hebrew*
9. purpose	*cleaning, reading*

- The adjectives *little, old,* and *young* are often used, not to give information, but as part of an adjective-noun combination. They are then placed next to their nouns, e.g., a nice little boy.
- Adjectives of personality and emotion come after adjectives of physical description (including *dark, fair, pale*), but before colours, e.g., a pale anxious traveller, an inquisitive black cat.
- Compound nouns are never separated by descriptive adjectives, e.g., step ladder, flower pot.

Exercise A

Write descriptive phrases by putting the following adjectives in appropriate order.

EXAMPLE: Chinese / warriors / 1.8 metre tall / distinctive / terracotta / thousands

thousands of 1.8 metre tall distinctive terracotta Chinese warriors

1. tropical / multi-coloured / schools / fish / salt water / small
2. sandy / clean / kilometres / beaches / white
3. stone / winding / wall / man-made / long
4. oriental / intriguing / ancient / culture / colourful
5. people / friendly / enthusiastic / nature-loving

Exercise B

Refer back to Marco's postcards. Identify the descriptive words or phrases and the type of adjectives used in the postcards.

EXAMPLE: great stone slabs
size / material / noun

2. Descriptive Techniques

There are other techniques writers use to provide readers with a clear and detailed visual picture.

- Organizing information spatially (usually from left to right, top to bottom, inside to outside) helps the reader visualize the whole picture.
- Using prepositional phrases helps the reader visualize the location of details.

EXAMPLE: *At the bottom* of Ayers Rock, you can see aboriginal paintings. As you climb *towards the middle* of the rock, the chain-link support that many people use to guide them abruptly ends. *Near the top*, the climb gets very steep and the air temperature plummets.

- Using words, phrases, and clauses that function as adjectives helps the reader visualize the details vividly.

EXAMPLE: At the bottom of Ayers Rock you can see *hundreds of ancient original rock paintings.*

Grammar In Use

1. Take a reader on a visit to a beautiful or famous landmark in your native country. Write at least ten descriptive sentences.
2. Write a postcard about a North American tourist attraction.
3. Write a descriptive paragraph based on one of the pictures on the following page.

Carnaval in Québec City.

Niagara Falls.

Lobster fishing on the east coast.

Before You Read

In teams of three or four, discuss the following questions.

1. A tourist usually visits popular sites that are well-known all over the world. An explorer, on the other hand, chooses to go to areas of the world well off the beaten path. If you could explore any part of the world, where would you go? Why?

2. You will read a journal entry from the book, *Paddle to the Amazon*, written by Don Starkell and Charles Wilkins. Don Starkell paddled a canoe over 19 000 km from Winnipeg to the Amazon with his two teenaged sons (only one son finished the voyage). This journey, a testament to perseverance and endurance, took them 23 months.

Look at the map outlining the route they took. What might you expect to see on this canoe trip?

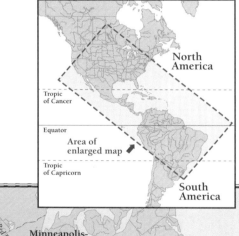

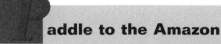

Paddle to the Amazon

May 5: in the Colson Cays, Belize

We have been advised by a number of fishermen and sailors not to paddle directly along the coast south of Belize City but to move out into the calmer waters of a long string of cays and islands that arches south
5 from here all the way to Guatemala. The only thing that bothers us is that the cays are anywhere from 10 to 18 miles [16 to 29 km] offshore.

Nevertheless, we paddled out and began island-hopping southwards. Our protective cays – small
10 islands formed of coral – are minuscule parts of the second largest coral reef on Earth, the largest being Australia's Great Barrier Reef.

By 3 p.m., we were tired and hungry and decided to make camp on the most southerly island of a little
15 group called the Colson Cays. The island was nothing to look at, just a little shelf of jagged coral protruding from the water. But on the north side of the island was a ramshackle fishing hut on stilts, in which we felt we could shelter for the night. The
20 shoreline was far too jagged for a landing, so we left the canoe loaded and in the water, tied to three posts that had been driven into the coral 6 or 7 feet [about

2 m] apart. With the sharp coral of the island so close, I put plenty of knots in the rope.

25 Our shack was in pretty grim shape, but we scraped the floor as clean as we could get it and moved in. But within an hour, the bugs were so bad inside, we moved back outside where there was a bit of breeze. Now, however, there was no place to sit comfortably, 30 so we moved 100 feet [30 m] to the other side of the island where a ratty little open-air biffy overhung the water. And there we spent the late afternoon, sitting side-by-side on the throne, Dana practising guitar, me writing.

35 With darkness coming on, we returned to the shack, tuned in Belize City on the radio, and ate a cold supper of corned beef, spaghetti, and black-eyed peas. By 11 p.m., Dana was asleep and I was in total darkness except for a tiny dot of red light from the 40 radio. At about midnight, the radio crackled sharply and went dead, though the red light still showed strongly, which was strange. I turned the set off and tried to sleep. But as I lay there, I began to feel uneasy.

I woke Dana, and we got up and looked out the 45 window. In spite of the darkness, we could see an incredible wall of storm clouds coming towards us from the south. But before we could do anything to prepare ourselves, lightning cracked out of the sky, and our little world was plunged into a chaos of wind 50 and rain, thunder and lightning.

In no time, our flimsy shelter was swaying and quivering on its 4-foot [1.2 m] stilts. We did our best to tie down the shutters and to tie the door shut, but there was nothing we could do about the crude siding 55 which was now flapping loose and started to pull away from the walls.

Only after several minutes did I fully come to my senses, remembering in a panic that the canoe was in the water just a few feet from the lethal coral bank. 60 But by this time there was nothing I could do about it. Our shack was tossing around in the gale, and Dana was frozen with fear.

A whole sheet of plywood siding was now ripped off the shack and whirled away, and Dana started 65 shouting, "We're going into the sea! We're going into the sea!" Sure enough, we could soon hear a watery roar beneath us. The huge waves were now washing

right across the island, tearing at the stilts of the shack.

70 For an hour or more, the storm raged, and the floor swayed beneath us. Then the wind died. It was all we could do to stare into the darkness in numbed silence. In time, I staggered to the door and stuck my head out. Unbelievably, the canoe was still there. I 75 could see its outline in the shallows.

Dana was soon up, and we dumped the water from the boxes and the canoe. As we packed up and retarped, we kept saying to one another, "It's a miracle ... I've never seen anything like it ... It's gotta be a 80 miracle ... It's just a miracle ... It *really* is a miracle ..."

(10) *minuscule*: extremely small, insignificant

(16) *jagged*: rough-edged

(18) *ramshackle*: about to fall to pieces

(18) *stilts*: pieces of wood used to support a building above the water

(31) *ratty*: badly worn

(31) *biffy*: outhouse (outdoor bathroom)

(49) *chaos*: state of total confusion

(51) *flimsy*: very thin and easily destroyed

(51) *swaying*: moving back and forth

(52) *quivering*: shaking

(59) *lethal*: deadly

(61) *gale*: very strong wind

(72) *numbed*: unable to feel anything

Comprehension Check

1. Why did the Starkells choose to paddle around the cays even though they were located far from the shoreline?

2. What were the major factors that determined how far they would paddle that day?

3. Approximately how wide was the island?

4. What are some key descriptive words that the writer uses to create a picture of how poorly constructed the shack was?

5. Make a list of the damage caused by the storm.

One Step Beyond

1. Why was the radio going silent a signal of approaching disaster?

2. Was the shack used frequently?

3. Why was the shack built on stilts?

4. The writer recognizes that his readers may be unfamiliar with the area he is describing in this journal entry. What evidence is there in the passage to support this?

5. Why did the Starkells consider their survival, and the survival of their canoe, as such a miracle?

Speaking

For information about local areas of interest, many people call a tourist information service before they go or ask local residents once they are in the area. Before setting out on his epic adventure, Don Starkell researched the route he and his sons would take and the places of interest they would see. One of the last major cities they would visit before leaving North America was New Orleans.

The following is a list of responses he would have received if he had called the tourist board before departing. What are the questions that he might have asked to get these responses?

EXAMPLE:

> *Response*: It takes place in February. Mardi Gras attracts tourists from all over the world.
>
> *Question*: When is Mardi Gras?

1. *Response:* Of course, Mardi Gras is just one of the annual attractions; however, there are many other attractions that are open all year round.

2. a) *Response:* One thing you certainly don't want to miss is the Audubon Zoo. It has a Louisiana swamp exhibit that lets you wander through a cypress swamp and view a rare white alligator. It also has a show of robotic prehistoric animals.

   b) *Response:* You can either take a streetcar or get there by boat from the French Quarter.

3. a) *Response:* The most unique thing to see is probably the Voodoo museum.

   b) *Response:* It's located at 724 Dumaine.

4. *Response:* The French Quarter is filled with unique shops as well as the best restaurants and hotels. It's alive with street tap-dancers, musicians, mimes, and portrait artists. You simply can't visit New Orleans without visiting the French Quarter.

5. *Response:* The Prince Conti is located in the French Quarter. It's a European-style hotel that has 50 guest rooms filled with antiques. I would also recommend Place D'Armes located at Jackson Square — it's classic yet casual.

6. *Response:* We're open from 9 a.m. to 5 p.m. If you think of any other questions, give us a call or visit our web site.

Now role play the telephone conversation with a partner. Then select another tourist destination and create a dialogue in which one person asks for specific information about the area and the other person provides it. Present the dialogue to the class.

Types of travellers	Examples/Names

Listening 1
T3.a

Before You Listen

Working in teams of four or five, discuss the following questions.

1. What sources of information did travellers have hundreds of years ago before they set off on their explorations?

2. Do you know of any famous women explorers? Who are they?

3. Why are accounts of male explorers more prevalent than those of female explorers?

4. Under what circumstances were women able to travel in the past? Compare this with today's opportunities for travel.

5. How does culture affect a woman's opportunity to travel or explore?

Focused Listening

Names of famous male explorers such as Christopher Columbus and Henry Hudson are familiar to many; however, there were many women in history who also explored new frontiers. You will hear a brief lecture about historic women travellers and their contributions. As you listen, complete the following chart.

The Shoshone woman Sacagawea was a famous guide and explorer.

Comprehension Check

Based on the lecture, complete the following sentences.

1. Women emigrants . . .

2. Religion prompted . . .

3. Women travellers of the 19th century prepared the way . . .

4. Women travelled to accompany . . .

5. Women did not have the same . . .

6. In the 19th century women travelled . . .

7. Women served . . .

For Discussion

1. How has the role of women travellers changed in the last 100 years? What main factors have contributed to this change?

2. The accomplishments of these women are very inspirational. What can we do to make future generations as aware of women's contributions to world exploration as they are of men's?

Places explored	Contribution

Vocabulary 1

1. Unscramble the adjectives in the following sentences. Use the context to help you.

   a) Mary Kingsley was a (*vaber*) _____ woman who travelled in Africa through the unknown country of the Fang people.

   b) Marguerite Baker Harrison was a (*gcrououesa*) _____ , (*vatruodneus*) _____ woman who served her country as a spy.

   c) The (*dddeteaci*) _____ Japanese women's climbing expedition reached the summit of Mt. Everest.

   d) Svetlana Savitskaya, a truly (*patlanosiniri*) _____ woman, was the first woman to walk in space.

   e) The (*srpreegniver*) _____ Naomi Jones sailed around the world alone in nine months in 1977/78.

2. The more precise your descriptive words are, the more accurate a picture you paint. Visualize a beautiful park and list three things you see. Then compare your items with a partner's. You will note that people interpret "beautiful" in different ways. Some may list colourful flowers, others children playing, and still others exotic birds or animals. The adjective "beautiful" is not very precise.

   Below are four rather general descriptive words. Brainstorm with a partner to find at least eight other words you could use in their place that would be more precise and descriptive. Think of appropriate nouns some of your new adjectives could describe and share your descriptions with other teams.

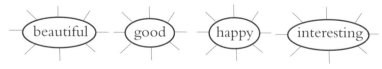

Writing

Write a journal entry describing a real or imaginary exploration – a journey in Antarctica, an ocean voyage, a journey through the desert, or a trek through the mountains, for example. Use precise descriptive words to create a clear picture.

Grammar Focus 2

RELATIVE CLAUSES

1. Defining Relative Clauses

Relative clauses are adjective clauses that identify or add additional information to a noun. *Who, whom, that, which,* and *whose* are relative pronouns used to introduce relative clauses.

The relative adverbs *when* (for time, sometimes replacing *on/in which*), *where* (for place, sometimes replacing *at/in which*), and *why* (replacing *for which*) may also introduce relative clauses but are less common.

EXAMPLES: I'll never forget the year (when) the first astronaut walked on the moon.
The astronauts raised a flag to mark the place (where) they landed.
Do you know the reason (why) people wanted to travel to the moon?

Exercise A

1. Read the following passage and underline the relative clauses.

Isabella Bird, whose married name was Bishop, was born in 1831 in Yorkshire, England. This was a time in history when religion played a very important part in people's lives. Under the influence of her father, who was a clergyman, she became a devout member of the Church of England. She believed that religions which differed from her own were based on harmful superstitions. As a youngster, Bird had extremely poor health that sometimes prevented her from getting out of bed. A doctor recommended travel to perk up her spirits. In 1854 she set out by steamship to visit Canada where her cousin lived.

During the trip her health improved tremendously. For the first time in her life she was on her own. This was a liberating experience for a Victorian woman. After visiting with her cousin a short while, she set off on a three-month tour that took her to Montreal, Toronto, Chicago, and New England. She travelled by train and by stagecoach along bumpy and rutted roads. Her family really enjoyed her lively and colourful letters, which described why she found her travels so inspirational. When she came home, she decided to turn her letters into a book, which was published in 1856.

2. Now based on your analysis of the passage, answer these questions.

a) Is each relative clause subordinate or independent? That is, can the relative clause stand on its own as a complete sentence or does it need to be attached to another clause for meaning?

b) Which words at the beginning of a relative clause are used to describe people, objects/conditions, possession, location, and time?

c) Why are some relative clauses set off by commas while others are not? Do the clauses set off by commas provide essential information?

2. Types of Relative Clauses

A relative clause is a dependent clause that cannot stand alone in a sentence; it must always be connected to an independent clause. The relative clause modifies a noun and must always be placed in the sentence directly after the noun it describes.

noun   relative
         pronoun

EXAMPLE: It's a (culture) **that** *is steeped in tradition.*

independent clause   relative clause

There are two main types of relative clauses – restrictive and non-restrictive. Each type has distinct meanings and uses.

3. Restrictive or Defining Relative Clauses

The restrictive or defining relative clause is essential in the sentence because it clearly identifies the noun. Without the information in the relative clause, the particular noun the writer is referring to may not be clear.

EXAMPLE: Women travellers *who accompanied their menfolk* explored unknown regions.

In this sentence, the writer is referring specifically to the women travellers who accompanied their menfolk, not *all* women travellers. The clause adds information essential to the understanding of the sentence.

Tip

The relative pronouns *who, whom, which,* and *that* can refer to singular or plural nouns. The relative pronoun does not change form.

When the relative pronouns *who, that,* or *which* come before the verb in the relative clause, they are subject relative pronouns because they act as the subject of the relative clause. Relative pronouns may also act as an object of a verb or preposition in a restrictive relative clause.

SUBJECT: The woman *who won the trip* was my aunt.
OBJECT: The newspaper *that I bought* contained the latest travel information.

The forms of the relative pronouns used in restrictive relative clauses are as follows:

	Subject	Object	Possessive
For persons	who that	whom/who that	whose
For things	which that	which that	whose/of which

- *whose* shows the relationship to a person, animal, or thing such as a country or an organization
- *whose* + noun can be the object of a preposition

EXAMPLE: Henry is the man *whose* car we rode in.
          Henry is the man in *whose* car we rode.

The second sentence is more formal.

- *of which* is used for things but is considered more formal than *whose*
- when the relative pronoun functions as the object of a verb or preposition in a restrictive relative clause, it can be omitted

EXAMPLE: The newspaper *I bought* contained the latest travel information.

Grammar Focus 2

Exercise B

Identify the relative clauses in the following sentences and determine whether the relative pronoun is acting as the subject, object, or possessive.

1. The backpacker that we gave a ride to is from Australia.
2. *Paddle to the Amazon* is about a man and his son who canoe from Winnipeg to the Amazon.
3. Marco is the person whose postcards we read.
4. Isabella Bird sold the stories which she wrote.
5. Have you visited the woman whom you met on your trip to France?
6. The travel magazine, the title of which I can't remember, provides useful information.

4. Non-Restrictive or Non-Defining Relative Clauses

Non-restrictive relative clauses are used after nouns that are already definite; as a result, rather than defining the noun, the clause adds additional information that is not necessary for the understanding of the sentence. This type of clause can easily be omitted and the reader would still understand which noun the author was referring to. A non-restrictive relative clause is always separated from the noun and the rest of the sentence by commas.

EXAMPLE: My mother, *who wrote to me often,* experienced my trip vicariously through my letters.

In this sentence, the omission of the relative clause would not change the meaning of the sentence since it is not necessary to the identification of *mother*. This type of sentence structure is considered fairly formal, and appears more frequently in written than in spoken English.

The forms of the relative pronouns in non-restrictive relative clauses are as follows:

	Subject	Object	Possessive
For persons	*who*	*whom/who*	*whose*
For things	*which*	*which*	*whose/of which*

- The relative pronoun *that* is not used in non-restrictive relative clauses.
- The relative pronoun can never be omitted in a non-restrictive relative clause.
- Prepositions can be placed before *whom* and *which*; however, this is formal usage.

Exercise C

Working in pairs, determine whether the clauses in the following sentences are restrictive or non-restrictive. If they are non-restrictive, add appropriate punctuation.

1. In the 1800s only a few Europeans managed to explore Tibet which is located on a high isolated plateau between China and India.
2. Tibet's religion, Buddhism, was ruled by a caste of high priests who were called lamas.
3. In 1892, the English missionary Annie Taylor who lived and worked in China was the first western woman to visit Little Tibet which was located on the southwestern border of Tibet proper.
4. Alexandra David-Neel was the first western woman to reach Lhasa. Reaching Lhasa which was both a geographical achievement and a spiritual adventure was accomplished in 1924.
5. In 1927, Alexandra David-Neel wrote a book that gained her recognition as the world's leading authority on Tibet. The book was called My *Journey to Lhasa.*

Exercise D

Combine the following sentences using relative clauses.

1. Fanny Bullock Workman made several cycling journeys through India and Southeast Asia. The bicycle journeys totalled 22 400 km.
2. In 1893 Mary Kingsley travelled to West Africa. She collected river fish there.
3. From 1931-1938, Louise Arnor Boyd led four expeditions to East Greenland. The expeditions were undertaken to make maps, take photographs, and collect plant specimens.
4. In 1975, a climbing expedition reached the summit of Mt. Everest. The expedition consisted of only Japanese women.

5. In 1979, Sylvia Earle reached the record-breaking depth of 380 m beneath the sea's surface. She was an American scientist and diver.

Grammar In Use

Restrictive relative clauses are used to identify, define, summarize, classify, explain, and provide new information. Write several sentences using restrictive relative clauses that give clues to an object, place, or person you are thinking of. Working in teams of four or five, read your sentences aloud and see if your teammates can guess what you are describing.

EXAMPLE: There is someone in this class *who lives there.*
It is a place *that used to be a British penal colony.*
It is a country *that is also a continent.*
It has a coral reef *which is the largest in the world.*
The kangaroo is one animal *that is well-known in this country.*
Answer: Australia

Reading 2

Susanna Moodie was an emigrant to Canada in the 1830s. She kept detailed notes of the hardships that she and her family faced trying to eek out a living in this new country. Based on her experiences, she wrote the well-known book *Roughing it in the Bush.* Her imaginative descriptions of place and character have been widely recognized as classic Canadian literature. You will read an excerpt that richly describes a view Susanna Moodie saw on a trip she took to an area along the St. Lawrence River.

A pioneer homestead in Upper Canada, 1830.

Before You Read

Working in teams of three or four, complete the following tasks.

a) Jot down some descriptive words or phrases that you might use to describe the picture.

b) Write a short paragraph describing the picture. Organize your ideas spatially giving clear visual cues, such as "to the left," "in the middle," "to the right of," etc.

c) Susanna Moodie describes a river with mountains in the background. List at least five adjectives that you might expect to find in the description.

Roughing it in the Bush

"What sublime views of the north side of the river those *habitants* of St. Thomas must enjoy," thought I. Perhaps familiarity with the scene has rendered them indifferent to its astonishing beauty.

5   Eastward, the view down the St. Lawrence towards the Gulf is the finest of all, scarcely surpassed by anything in the world. Your eyes follow the long range of lofty mountains until their blue summits are blended and lost in the blue of the sky. Some of 10 these, partially cleared round the base, are sprinkled over with neat cottages, and the green slopes that spread around them are covered with flocks and herds. The surface of the splendid river is diversified with islands of every size and shape, some in wood, 15 others partially cleared, and adorned with orchards and white farmhouses. As the early sun streamed upon the most prominent of these, leaving the others in deep shade, the effect was strangely novel and imposing. In more remote regions, where the forest 20 has never yet echoed to the woodman's axe, or received the impress of civilization, the first approach to the shore inspires a melancholy awe which becomes painful in its intensity.

> *And silence — awful silence broods*
> *Profoundly o'er these solitudes;*
> *Not but the lapsing of the floods*
> *Breaks the deep stillness of the woods;*
> *A sense of desolation reigns*
> *O'er these unpeopled forest plains*
> *Where sounds of life ne'er wake a tone*
> *Of cheerful praise round Nature's throne,*
> *Man finds himself with God — alone.*

Comprehension Check

Susanna Moodie's language is extremely rich with description. Each sentence is carefully crafted to evoke detailed pictures in the reader's mind. Match the descriptive phrases Susanna Moodie has used in Column 1 below with the plainer and less formal descriptions in Column 2.

Column 1	Column 2
1. received the impress of civilization	a) a bunch of high mountains
2. the forest has never yet echoed to the woodman's axe	b) there were several different-sized islands in the river
3. scarcely surpassed by anything	c) there were many sheep and cattle
4. long range of lofty mountains	d) interesting and memorable
5. sprinkled over with neat cottages	e) no trees have ever been cut down in that forest
6. covered with flocks and herds	f) hardly anything is better
7. diversified with islands of every shape and size	g) touched by people
8. adorned with orchards and white farmhouses	h) small cottages are scattered
9. strangely novel and imposing	i) covered with orchards and farmhouses

For Discussion

1. In teams of three or four reread the passage, substituting the simpler phrases from Column 2. (You may have to change them slightly to fit grammatically). Discuss the effect this has on the description.

2. What words or phrases has Susanna Moodie used to indicate that her description is following a specific sequence, that is, left to right or top to bottom, etc.?

One Step Beyond

1. Susanna Moodie ends the description with a poem. Why? What effect does it have on the reader?

2. In what types of writing would richly descriptive language like Susanna Moodie's be appropriate? In what types of writing would it be inappropriate?

3. Why is it important to use spatial descriptors when describing a scene?

 istening 2   T3.b

Women travellers of the 19th century stretched the boundaries established for women by challenging their traditional roles and pushing the limits of their abilities. They set the groundwork for the future achievements of women in exploration and in other fields.

In this century Canadian astronaut Roberta Bondar has expanded women's roles further by becoming Canada's first female astronaut in space. Her impressive list of academic credentials includes a Bachelor of Science in Zoology and Agriculture, a Master of Science, a Doctorate in Neurobiology, and a Doctorate in Medicine. Her studies and research on the nervous system made her the ideal candidate for Canada's astronaut program when it was established in 1983. Roberta Bondar became the first Canadian woman in space on January 22, 1992, after many years of training. On the mission she was designated as a Payload Specialist and conducted experiments in the space lab. Since leaving the space program, she has continued to serve as a role model for future generations.

You will hear an interview between five 10-year-old children and Dr. Roberta Bondar.

Before You Listen

In teams of three or four, discuss the following questions.

1. What kinds of questions would you expect 10-year-olds to ask Dr. Bondar? Do you think adults would ask different questions?

2. How might seeing planet Earth from space change your view of the world?

3. Do you think that space travel in the next century will be as common as air travel is in your lifetime?

For Discussion

After listening to the interview, discuss the following questions in teams.

1. Who might Peter Pan be? Why is this an appropriate example to use with a group of 10-year-olds?

2. What impact did seeing Earth from space have on Dr. Bondar?

3. Dr. Bondar is asked a question about God at the end of the interview that she doesn't want to answer. How does she handle this?

One Step Beyond

1. Dr. Bondar mentions that being weightless is like being a bird. How does weightlessness present challenges for astronauts in space?

2. How can parents help their children realize their childhood dreams?

3. Rewrite the interview imagining that the questions are asked by adults. How would Dr. Bondar's answers and her language be different?

Speaking

On a space flight, you and your fellow astronauts discovered a small inhabited planet hidden behind the moon. In a short three- to five-minute presentation, describe the planet (its inhabitants, atmosphere, vegetation, etc.).

Writing

Write a short descriptive essay on one of the following topics.

- the changes in exploration over the last 200 years
- the similarities and differences between Susanna Moodie's and Roberta Bondar's explorations
- how Susanna Moodie and Roberta Bondar each explored new frontiers
- the importance of the space program
- the experience of looking down on Earth from space

A view of the Earth from space.

Unit Reflection

Based on the contents of this unit, discuss the meaning of the title "The Road Less Travelled." What applications might this phrase have beyond a physical journey?

Unit 4

That's Not What I Meant

DISCUSSION

1. Explain the message of each cartoon.
2. What do all the cartoons have in common?
3. Look at the Cathy cartoon. In what ways do you think men and women communicate differently?

DENNIS THE MENACE

"MR. WILSON REALLY LOVES THAT WATCH YOU GAVE HIM. HE'S ALWAYS LOOKIN' AT IT WHEN I'M HERE!"

PEANUTS reprinted by permission of United Features Syndicate, Inc.

Vocabulary 1

1. The idioms below are all associated with communication. Match those in Column A with their meanings in Column B.

Column A	Column B
a) to get to the point (of)	1. to force or pressure someone to provide details
b) to miss the point (of)	2. to start talking about a topic that is different from the original purpose or subject of conversation
c) to get off track / to get sidetracked	3. to not understand the specific idea expressed
d) to beat around the bush	4. to hear (something) from someone who heard it from someone else
e) to pin (someone) down (on something)	5. to avoid making a direct (clear) statement
f) to hear (it) through the grapevine or to hear through the grapevine that . . .	6. to say what is most important

2. Fill in the blanks with an appropriate form of the idiom. Pay attention to the required tense.

GIRLFRIEND: Honey, you're not listening to me again.

BOYFRIEND: I am listening, but you're just going on and on. Why don't you just _____?

GIRLFRIEND: Alright! Alright! I'm just trying to _____ you _____ on your plans for the future as far as it concerns us.

BOYFRIEND: You're _____ again. Why don't you just come out and ask. You want to know if I'm going to marry you.

GIRLFRIEND: Okay. Do you want to marry me?

BOYFRIEND: Look. Neither of us is settled into a secure job yet and I'm a little unsure about my future. And what about you? Didn't you want to go to graduate school? By the way, have you heard anything yet about getting accepted?

GIRLFRIEND: Forget about that. Let's not _____. I asked you specifically if you want to get married.

BOYFRIEND: It's not that I don't want to marry you. It's just that this isn't the right time. Listen. I've _____ that Professor Stanson may be leaving the department. I think I have a good chance to get his job. If I do get the job, it'll mean a lot of work in the beginning. So this just isn't a good time to think of marriage. Do you get my point?

GIRLFRIEND: Oh I get your point. But you've_____ my _____. I want to settle down and start a family. We've been dating for six years already and I'm not willing to wait another five years.

Listening 1

T4.a

Sociolinguist Dr. Deborah Tannen is the author of *You Just Don't Understand*, a provocative book that explores the differences in the conversational styles of men and women. You will hear excerpts of Dr. Tannen's book.

Excerpt 1

Before You Listen

Sometimes simple conversations turn into arguments because of miscommunication. Think about the last "silly" argument you had with a peer of the opposite sex (a boyfriend, girlfriend, or a classmate) and discuss what happened in the conversation that turned it into an argument.

Focused Listening

Listen to this conversation between Maureen and Philip who are trying to set a date for a dinner party. Then answer the questions.

1. What happens on the weekend of October 10 that influences the decision about the date of the dinner party?

2. Why does Maureen ask Philip whether he wouldn't want to hunt later on the Saturday, after he has just agreed to setting the date of the party on the Saturday?

3. Why does her question annoy Philip?

One Step Beyond

1. What causes the argument?

2. Compare what happens in this conversation to what happened in the argument you discussed earlier. Describe the similarities and differences between this argument and the one you had.

Excerpt 2

Before You Listen

Work in small mixed male/female groups. Take turns describing yourself to the group. Once every team member has finished, discuss how comfortable you were doing this.

Focused Listening

Listen to this fictional dialogue which illustrates another difference in how men and women communicate. Then answer the questions.

1. What do you know about Johan based on his description of himself?

2. What do you know about Marianne based on her description of herself?

One Step Beyond

1. What were some of the obvious differences between how Johan and Marianne answered the interviewer's questions?

2. Who do you think is the dominant partner in this relationship? Give reasons for your answer.

3. Why do you think Marianne has such a difficult time describing herself?

4. What is your impression of Johan's character?

5. This is a fictional conversation from a movie. Do you think it bears any relation to the way men and women communicate in reality? If so, how? If not, why not?

Excerpt 3

Before You Listen

Think back to when you were a young child in the first few years at school. What kinds of games did you and your friends like to play? Were there differences in the ways that boys and girls played?

Focused Listening

Listen to this excerpt which describes research on how men and women learn different ways of speaking even in early childhood. Then answer these questions.

1. What evidence is there to support the idea that children learn to talk not only from their parents but also from their peers?

2. How are boys' games organized?

3. How are girls' games organized?

4. Listen again and complete the following chart comparing specific aspects of boys' and girls' games.

One Step Beyond

1. This excerpt was based on research conducted in the United States. If such research were conducted in your native culture, do you think the results would be the same? What would be similar? What would be different?

2. What relationship may there be between how girls and boys learn to use language as they are growing up and how they communicate with each other as adults?

3. Discuss the meaning of the term *stereotype*. Do you think that the information presented in this excerpt may promote stereotypes? Why or why not?

4. One way to avoid stereotyping is to consider examples that counter the beliefs about a particular group. Have you made any observations about boys and girls in play that counter the research findings? Be specific.

 Writing

Based on the information in the listening activity, write a paragraph about the differences in girls' and boys' games.

	Boys	Girls
What is most important in their games?		
How do they achieve status?		
How do they communicate in their games?		

Grammar Focus 1

CONJUNCTIONS AND PREPOSITIONS OF CONTRAST

Effective communicators clearly show how their ideas are related to one another. For example, they may show that ideas are obviously different by joining them using conjunctions and transitions of contrast.

EXAMPLE: Women are more likely to tell jokes in small, same-sex groups, (whereas) men are more likely to tell jokes in large, mixed-sex groups.

In this sentence, the conjunction *whereas* connects contrasting ideas about how men and women tell jokes.

1. Coordinating Conjunctions of Contrast

(but   yet)

But and *yet* are two common coordinating conjunctions that show contrast. Coordinating conjunctions connect sentence parts that are grammatically the same. For example, the conjunction may connect or show the relationship between two words or phrases.

SINGLE WORDS: Their argument was *brief* (but) *damaging.*

PHRASES: Men and women *speak the same language* (yet) *communicate very differently.*

Coordinating conjunctions may also connect two similar clauses, such as two dependent or two independent clauses. A dependent clause is a group of words with a subject and verb, but it does not make sense on its own and cannot stand alone as a sentence. An independent clause is a group of words with a subject and a verb that makes sense on its own and can stand alone as a sentence. A comma is often placed before the co-ordinating conjunction to separate longer clauses. Shorter clauses are often connected without commas.

DEPENDENT CLAUSES: Some women feel they have to be aggressive *when they speak with men* (but not) *when they speak with other women.*

INDEPENDENT CLAUSES: When women tell men their problems *they don't usually want men to solve the problems,* (yet) *men believe that they have to offer solutions.*

Exercise A

Complete the following sentences using coordinating conjunctions of contrast.

1. Boys and girls grow up in the same neighbourhoods,
   but . . .
   yet . . .

2. Parents speak to both their sons and daughters,
   but . . .
   yet . . .

3. Gender stereotypes are still evident today,
   but . . .
   yet . . .

2. Subordinate Conjunctions of Contrast in Adverb Clauses

(although   though
even though   while   whereas
in spite of the fact that)

Subordinate conjunctions connect a subordinate (dependent) clause to a main (independent) clause. The subordinate conjunction is always found at the beginning of the dependent clause.

EXAMPLE: *subordinate (dependent) clause*

(Although) they may not introduce as many new topics into a conversation as women, *men may interrupt more during a conversation.*

main (independent) clause

Punctuation of a Dependent Clause

The dependent clause can be placed:

a) before the independent clause (followed by a comma which separates the two clauses)

(Although) they may not introduce as many new topics into a conversation as women, *men may interrupt more during a conversation.*

b) within the independent clause (with a comma before and after the dependent clause)

Men, (although) *they may not introduce as many new topics into a conversation as women,* may interrupt more during a conversation.

c) after the independent clause (no comma separates the clauses). Subordinate clauses with *while* are usually placed before the independent clause.

Men may interrupt more during a conversation (although) *they may not introduce as many new topics into a conversation as women.*

Exercise B

The following list of gender talk differences has been researched and compiled by Lillian Glass in her book *He Says, She Says*. Use the information in the list to write sentences that show contrast. Try to use different subordinate conjunctions. (You may also get into a lively discussion about whether you agree or disagree with these statements!)

Men

1) They take up more physical space when sitting or standing, with arms and legs stretched out away from their bodies.

2) They gesture away from the body.

3) They provide less listener feedback through their body language.

4) In general, they touch others more often.

5) They tend to avoid eye contact and do not look directly at the other person.

6) They mumble words more and have sloppier pronunciation.

7) They talk at a slower rate of speech.

8) They get to the point more quickly.

9) They use more slang words and jargon.

10) They use more teasing and sarcasm to show affection.

11) They laugh and giggle less.

12) They see time as having a beginning, a middle, and an end.

13) They talk more about themselves and their accomplishments.

14) They gossip less.

15) They do not often apologize after a confrontation.

Women

1) They take up less physical space when sitting, with arms and legs toward their bodies.

2) They gesture toward the body.

3) They provide more listener feedback through their body language.

4) They touch others less often.

5) They tend to look more directly at another person and have better eye contact.

6) They use quicker and more precise articulation and better pronunciation.

7) They talk at a faster rate of speech.

8) They tend to beat around the bush more often.

9) They use fewer slang words and jargon.

10) They use little sarcasm and teasing to show affection.

11) They laugh and giggle more.

12) They see time as flowing more continuously.

13) They talk more about other people's accomplishments and minimize their own.

14) They gossip more.

15) They often apologize after a confrontation.

3. In spite of / Despite

We can use the prepositions *in spite of /despite* with a noun phrase or an *ing* verbal. The meaning is similar to that of *although* + *clause*.

EXAMPLES: Men and women can learn to communicate effectively with each other, (in spite of/ despite) the differences in their conversational styles.

(In spite of / Despite) growing up in the same neighbourhood, boys and girls grow up in different worlds of words.

Exercise C

Using the information in Exercise B, write five sentences using *in spite of /despite*.

Grammar In Use

Write an essay contrasting the communication styles of men and women. Include information about body language, voice and speech patterns, and conversation patterns.

Speaking

The differences in the communication styles of men and women can cause a communication gap or breakdown. However, as the cartoons at the beginning of the unit suggest, factors other than gender can also cause communication problems. In small groups, brainstorm five to ten other barriers to effective communication. Share your ideas with other groups.

Vocabulary 2

1. Match the words in Column A with their definitions in Column B.

Column A	Column B
a) interaction	1. body movements
b) barriers	2. not clearly expressed
c) feedback	3. interpretation of an idea
d) interpersonal	4. expressed clearly and with few words
e) gestures	5. a response with your opinion
f) perception	6. between people
g) vague	7. problems or obstacles
h) message	8. information sent to a person, group, etc.
i) cue	9. signal
j) concise	10. communication or dealings between people

2. Match each word in the list below with a preposition that is often used with it. You may use a preposition more than once. Then write a sentence for each word and preposition combination. Check your answers with a partner.

interaction	barriers
feedback	perception

to	between	on	of

Reading 1

Before You Read

You will read an article about cross-cultural communication.

Just as gender (male/female) communication styles differ, cultural communication styles also differ. In teams, discuss some of your experiences with the differences in the way North Americans communicate and people from your native culture communicate.

Learning ways North Americans communicate can lead to fun moments in the classroom.

Anticipating Information

Now begin reading the article below. After you read the anecdote (story) that begins the article, stop.

Communicating Across Cultures

1. Hoa has just arrived from Vietnam. Her cousin Phuong and some of his American friends are waiting at the airport to greet her. Hoa and Phuong are both excited about this meeting because they have been separated for seven years. As soon as Hoa enters the passenger terminal, Phuong introduces her to his friends Tom, Don, and Charles. Tom steps forward and hugs and kisses Hoa. She pushes him away and bursts into tears.

Discussion

Based on this anecdote, discuss what you think this reading will be about. Then read the next section.

2. Imagine Tom's surprise at this reaction. By American standards Tom did the right thing. As a good friend of Phuong's he shared in the excitement and anticipation of Hoa's arrival. To show how happy he was to meet her and to welcome her warmly, he hugged and kissed her. So why did Hoa reject his sign of welcome?

Unfortunately, Tom didn't understand that in Hoa's culture such gestures in this situation are not a sign of welcome, but a sign of disrespect for a young woman. Among Chinese from Vietnam, if a boy hugs and kisses a girl in public, he insults her. Chinese culture in Vietnam is very strict about this, especially in the rural areas where Hoa grew up. She described her village: "After children are ten years old, boys and girls cannot play together. A boy and girl cannot date without their parents' approval. A man and woman cannot hug or kiss if they're not married."

In Hoa's village if anyone violated these rules, the villagers punished the girl by forcing her to kneel on the ground so they could spit at her and throw rocks at her. No wonder that Phuong's American friends frightened Hoa. She did not know what punishment for public hugging and kissing might be meted out to her in this country.

Eventually Hoa learned to be comfortable when greeted with hugs and kisses, accepting them as merely perfunctory acts.

Comprehension Check

1. In the village where Hoa grew up, what happened once boys and girls reached the age of ten?

2. What was the punishment in Hoa's village for girls who violated these social rules?

3. What do you think is the meaning of the phrase "accepting them as merely perfunctory acts" in the last paragraph?

Discussion

What main point do you think this reading is going to make?

3. There were two communication forces that influenced the interaction between Hoa and Tom. Firstly, Tom communicated his message through body language. Perhaps he did this because of language barriers, but more likely he did what comes naturally to most of us. He instinctively communicated with his body.

We mistakenly believe that most of our messages are conveyed through words, but research confirms that almost 97% of a message's impact is conveyed through non-verbal cues. Consequently, what we communicate with our bodies and voices is as important as what we communicate with our words. A nod of the head, a wink of the eye, a simple hand movement, a sincere smile or an intrusion of personal space can say more than many words, and it can certainly have a greater impact.

Discussion

One of the communication forces that influenced this interaction was body language. What do you think the other influencing factor was? Explain the reasons for your answer.

4. The second factor that contributed to the communication mishap has to do with culture. Tom didn't know very much about Hoa's culture and, conversely, Hoa didn't understand American culture. Consequently, both of them interpreted the body gestures according to their own cultural norms. Unfortunately, these two cultures interpret these gestures very differently.

Many aspects of culture – languages, beliefs, rules, customs, myths, family patterns, and political and economic systems determine how we communicate, both verbally and non-verbally. With such a diversity in beliefs, customs, and social systems, it is not difficult to understand that how people use body language to communicate will vary from one culture to another.

Comprehension Check

1. What aspects of culture affect how we communicate?

2. Which sentence in this section gives a clue about what you will read in the next section?

Discussion

Think of two examples from your own experience that illustrate how the same body language is used and interpreted differently in different cultures. Make a point-form outline of a paragraph that you could insert here to support the last statement in the section above. Begin your paragraph with "For example, . . ."

How are greetings different in various cultures?

5. Not only is touching in public with someone of the opposite sex offensive in the Chinese culture of Vietnam, but in other cultures as well. Muslim taboos regarding interaction between non-related members of the opposite sex prevent men and women not only from hugging and kissing in public, but from engaging in any relationship outside of marriage. In Malaysia and other Islamic countries, the head is believed to contain sacred spiritual and intellectual powers and should never be touched. On the other hand, there are cultures where body contact is not only permitted, but expected. When greeting, most Latinos expect body contact. Hugging and kissing on the cheek are acceptable for both the same sex and the opposite sex. How we communicate through eye contact also varies from culture to culture. Most North Americans are uncomfortable with the suggested intimacy of prolonged direct eye contact. Yet extended eye contact is very common in Arab cultures. Arabs believe the eyes are the windows to the soul and that looking into someone's eyes helps you to see what is in their heart. Avoiding direct eye contact in this culture communicates impoliteness, and insincerity. In Japan, however, children are taught never to look directly at someone who has superior status, such as a teacher. These are only examples of two types of body language that are used and interpreted differently around the world. There are many more.

Comprehension Check

1. Why is head touching taboo in Malaysia and other Islamic countries?

2. How is eye contact interpreted differently in Arab countries as compared to Japan?

3. Why are Americans uncomfortable with prolonged eye contact?

Discussion

This reading will now come to an end. How do you think the writer might end this reading?

6. Just as Hoa and Tom's lack of understanding of what and how different cultures communicate through body language resulted in a communication blunder, our own lack of understanding can lead us to sometimes serious miscommunication. Learning to communicate in another language then means much more than learning new words and grammar; it means learning how to use a range of communication signals, such as body language, in a cultural context. And, while it is certainly important for students of North American English to learn how body language is used to communicate ideas in this culture, learning how other cultures use body language is equally important for North Americans if they are to become effective communicators in today's shrinking world.

Comprehension Check

1. What does it mean to learn to communicate in another language?

2. Which sentence in this section states the main point of this reading?

One Step Beyond

1. What role does the anecdote about Hoa and Tom play in this reading?

2. How does the writer make the transition between the anecdote and the essay?

3. How does the writer connect the opening anecdote to the main point of the reading?

Writing

1. In section five of the reading, the writer uses touching and eye contact as examples of body language that is used and interpreted differently around the world. Based on the point-form outline you prepared in the reading, replace section five with a new paragraph using your own examples.

2. Using an anecdote to illustrate a main point in an essay is a very useful technique. Like a story, an anecdote has a beginning, a middle, and an end. It must also have a major point which is often placed at the end to complete the story. Think about a communication problem based on cultural differences that you have experienced or heard about. Write an anecdote that makes a specific point.

3. Write a journal entry about the major differences between communication in your native culture and North American culture.

Speaking

Charades

Work in teams of four to six. Each student on the team should try to send a short message without speaking (that is, using body language only). The first student to guess the message correctly becomes the next to "perform" another message. Continue this activity until each student has created at least two messages. Here is a list of messages to get you started:

Hello.	Hi.
Yes.	No way.
I don't understand.	You can't be serious.
Be quiet.	Be quiet!
Help!	How much?
See you later.	Good job!
Come here.	Are you crazy?
Could you repeat that?	This is disgusting.
What is this?	Cool.
I don't feel well.	Do you have the time?
I agree.	I'm not sure I agree.
I completely disagree.	I don't trust you.
I love this!	I'm so excited.

Grammar Focus 2

TRANSITION WORDS AND PHRASES OF CONTRAST

> however   still
> nevertheless   nonetheless   on the contrary*
> even so   on the other hand

Like coordinating conjunctions, transition words and phrases connect the ideas in independent clauses. They cannot, however, join single words, phrases, or dependent clauses.

*on the contrary is usually used to join ideas that are clearly opposite and cannot always be interchanged with the other conjunctive adverbs

EXAMPLES: This is one example of how cultures use body language differently to express an idea. (However), there are others.

(transition joining two ideas in separate sentences – two independent clauses)

This is one example; (however), there are others.
(transition joining ideas in two independent clauses)

Punctuation of Transitional Expressions

There are four patterns for punctuating transitional words:

1. transition word between two sentences (preceded by a semi-colon and followed by a comma)

Knowing how to speak the language is a start; (however), it is not enough.

2. transition word at the beginning of the second sentence (preceded by a period, capitalized, and followed by a comma)

   Knowing how to speak the language is a start. (However), it is not enough.

3. transition word within the second sentence (preceded and followed by a comma)

   Knowing how to speak the language is a start. It is, (however), not enough.

Unlike in this example, the transition word is usually placed after the complete subject but before the main verb.

4. transition word at the end of the second sentence (preceded by a comma and followed by a period)

   Knowing how to speak the language is a start. It is not enough, (however).

Note that the phrases *on the contrary, on the other hand*, and *even so* cannot be placed at the end of the second sentence.

Exercise A

however   still
nevertheless   nonetheless   on the contrary
even so   on the other hand

There are subtle differences in meaning among these transitional expressions. Discuss each word or expression with your classmates or look it up in the dictionary to find its specific meaning.

Exercise B

Work with a partner. Join the ideas in the following pairs of sentences to clearly show a contrastive relationship. Try to use as many different contrastive conjunctions and expressions as possible.

1. Many people believe that most of the impact of a message is conveyed through words. Research has shown that almost 97% of a message's impact is conveyed through non-verbal communication.

2. We don't know how much space any individual person needs to communicate comfortably. We do know what happens when this space is threatened.

3. Girls are more likely to say, "I'm sorry" than boys. Some research suggests that they are often less sorry when they make a mistake.

4. Her knowledge of English grammar was excellent. Her heavy accent remained a barrier to communication.

5. Technology hasn't made communicating easier. It has made it more difficult.

6. Word processing lets you revise text more easily. It can't teach you how to write more effectively.

7. Technology doesn't mean an improvement in the quality of life. Sometimes it means a worse quality of life.

8. We may think we are good listeners. Most of us are poor listeners.

9. We usually think of communication as spoken messages. Experts divide communication into two categories: verbal and non-verbal communication.

10. Some experts question how effective technology has been in improving communication. One cannot argue that the way in which we communicate has changed significantly with the introduction of technologies such as cellular phones.

Grammar In Use

Read the two opposing opinions about the use of language in communication. Then write as many contrastive sentences as you can.

Opinion #1

I am appalled at the lack of proper grammar and the simplification of writing and vocabulary evident in English today. Students seem to have forgotten (or to have never learned) basic sentence structure and punctuation. Essays are no more than a group of unrelated, poorly developed paragraphs (if you're lucky) that are laborious to read and cause serious miscommunication. Yet, students do not have a monopoly on poor language. Newspapers and magazines are full of grammar and spelling errors. It is time we began to teach young people how to communicate effectively in this wonderful language called English. We must (dare I say it) teach students grammar and, if need be, drill them. We must refuse to accept poorly written papers on any subject. We must not tolerate any spelling errors in written work. Our students deserve the best. When we do not train students to use and manipulate grammar, punctuation, and vocabulary to articulate their ideas, we are, in fact, denying them freedom of expression.

Opinion #2

I am fed up with all the criticism about the lack of proper English used today. When are academics and the "language elite" going to realize that English is changing? Most people accept the idea that Middle English (1150-1500) is irrelevant in today's world. Why is it so hard for people to accept that the English of our grandparents' day is becoming less relevant with each year? All languages have evolved over time – their grammar has changed, their pronunciation has changed, and their vocabulary has changed. That's the wonderful thing about language; it's a living form of expression. For goodness sake, the whole world is changing before our very eyes – economic structures are changing, political systems are changing, and the way we communicate is changing. Why shouldn't English be changing too? We not only need new words to express new ideas, we need new structures too. English has become a global language. Many people communicate internationally in English (as a second language) in industries ranging from transportation and medicine to mining and construction. And the English used globally is a new, evolving English. While it is true that we need a standard English to reduce miscommunication, there is no rule that says the standards of modern English can't change. The turmoil surrounding the use of a standard English doesn't stem from its death, but from its evolution.

Reading 2

Before You Read

You will read a short magazine article that describes how to improve your listening skills. But first, try the following questionnaire.

HOW GOOD A LISTENER ARE YOU?

To what extent do you exhibit the following listening behaviours?

	Often	Sometimes	Never
1. Prejudging topics and listening situations as unimportant, dry, or boring	☐	☐	☐
2. Criticizing a speaker's appearance or delivery	☐	☐	☐
3. Getting ego-involved with subjects and letting your emotions get involved	☐	☐	☐
4. Listening only for facts (while overlooking intent, purpose, or structure of a message)	☐	☐	☐
5. Trying to outline everything when taking notes	☐	☐	☐
6. Faking attention to the speaker	☐	☐	☐
7. Tolerating or creating distractions during communication activities (e.g., turning on the television while talking at the dinner table)	☐	☐	☐
8. Avoiding messages that are difficult to understand	☐	☐	☐
9. Reacting to specific words rather than the broader concept in a message (for instance, words like "abortion" that trigger word reactions)	☐	☐	☐
10. Letting your mind wander when you can somewhat follow what a speaker is saying	☐	☐	☐

How many times did you mark the "often" column? Assess your listening strengths and weaknesses.

Discussion

The questionnaire lists ten barriers to effective listening. In teams, write "key" words or phrases that define the barriers. Then, brainstorm one or two strategies for each barrier that will help you improve your listening skills. Share your strategies with the class.

Reading For Information

Now read the article below. Look for strategies to deal with the barriers listed in the quiz.

Want to Do Better on the Job? — LISTEN UP

This brief article gives useful suggestions for listening more effectively in business settings. The suggestions can easily be applied to the classroom or the home as well.

When Linda S., an Ohio banking executive, learned she would not be promoted she asked her boss why. He had barely begun to speak when she blurted out, "I know that whatever the reason I can do better!"

5　Exasperated, he replied, "You always interrupt before you even know what I'm going to say! How can you do better if you never listen?"

"Most people value speaking — which is seen as active — over listening, which is seen as passive," 10 explains Nancy Wyatt, professor of speech communication at Penn State University and co-author with Carol Ashburn of *Successful Listening* (Harper and Row, 1988).

And there are other reasons we might fail to tune in.

15　We may become so fixed on what we think that we tune out important information. Or we may react emotionally to a phrase or style the speaker uses and miss the main point. Or we're just too busy to pay attention to what is being said.

20　Sound familiar? If so, listen up, for changing your ways will pay big dividends. You'll stop wasting time on misunderstood assignments at work. People will start to see you as a perceptive, smart, and sensitive person who understands their needs. And that will 25 open new opportunities on the job suggests Lyman K. Steil, Ph.D., president of Communication Development Inc., a consulting firm based in St. Paul, Minn.

You can also develop an ear for the crucial but 30 unspoken words in conversation that signal problems in your business relationships.

Here are some suggestions for learning to listen to what is said — and not said — more effectively.

Control distractions: Give a speaker your full attention 35 or you're likely to miss the main point.

Identify the speaker's purpose: Tune into the speaker's agenda. Is he or she there to let off steam, solve a problem, share information, or just schmooze? Once you know, you can respond in the way he or she wants and expects. Learning to listen may also keep you from inadvertently getting caught in the cross fire of office politics.

Don't finish other people's sentences: Many people have this bad habit. Just observe yourself: Do you cut people off before they finish a thought? Are you so busy thinking about what you want to say you can't resist breaking in?

   "That often happens because the interrupter is bright, thinks she has grasped the point, and wants to show off how much she knows," says Dee Soder, Ph.D., president of Endymion, a New York City-based executive consulting firm. "What happens instead is that interrupters are perceived as being arrogant and interested only in themselves."

   To break the habit of interruption, bite your tongue and follow up with your comments only after the other person has had his or her say. Soder suggests you might even have to literally sit on your hands to keep your gestures from speaking for you.

   Finally, if you're not certain that the speaker has finished, ask!

Don't let the speaker's style turn you off: It's easy to tune out when less-than-favourite speakers clear their throats. One high school teacher confesses that for a long time she found a colleague's slow, deliberate drawl so grating that she simply could not listen to him. "It was only when I was forced to work with him and had to concentrate on *what* he was saying rather than how that I realized how smart and helpful he was and now we're best friends at work."

Don't be distracted by buzzwords: What springs to mind when you hear the label "feminist" or "right-to-lifer?" If you're like most people emotions take over and you stop paying careful attention to the point a speaker is trying to make.

Listen for what is not being said: Sometimes it's important to "hear between the lines." "Many people like to avoid conflict and so the person speaking is very reluctant to say anything negative," says Soder.

   When you suspect that a delicate or negative subject is being studiously avoided, you have to be prepared to delve deeper and ask the speaker, "Tell me more about that. Could you please explain?"

Show you are listening: Think about what your body language is revealing. Are you making good eye contact and leaning slightly forward in a way that indicates "I'm open to what you're saying?" Or are you tapping your foot and looking out to the window as if to say, "I have more important things to do than listen to you?"

Make a note of it: Jotting down a word or two can remind you later of the main purpose behind the assignment your boss is giving you.

   A brief note can also help you remember the point you would like to raise after the speaker finishes. For example, jot down "money" if you don't hear a potential employer mention it in an otherwise complete job description.

Make sure you heard it right: Many misunderstandings could be prevented if we'd just make sure we heard what we thought we heard. So when in doubt don't be afraid to ask, "Let me make sure I understand what you're saying." It's a hearing test well worth taking.

---

(21) *pay big dividends:* give you great rewards

(37) *let off steam:* complain without expecting a solution

(38) *schmooze:* have an intimate conversation

(41) *inadvertently:* without intention

(62) *turn (someone) off:* make (someone) disinterested in you

(66) *find (something) grating:* find (something) annoying

Comprehension Check

1. In the anecdote that introduces the article, what example of a communication blunder do we see Linda S. making?

2. What example illustrates how we can control the effect of interruptions?

3. According to Dee Soder, why do many people interrupt?

4. In what situation might the listener have to delve deeper and ask for more information?

5. How can you show someone that you are listening?

6. How can we make sure we've understood what the speaker has said?

One Step Beyond

1. The article makes suggestions about improving communication at work. How might you apply these suggestions to communication in your family?

2. Work individually or with a partner. Based on the information and suggestions in the article, design a brochure on "Effective Listening" using your own words.

peaking

Working in teams of three, choose a controversial topic with two opposing views, e.g., "Smoking should be banned from all public places." While two people have a short conversation of about three to five minutes in which one partner argues for the statement and the other against it, the third person acts as observer. After one person speaks, however, the partner must paraphrase (in his/her own words) what the speaker has just said before presenting his or her own view. The observer checks that the ideas are paraphrased accurately, assists if anything either partner says is misunderstood, and reports on the conversation to the class.

EXAMPLE: Topic – Communication on the internet should be regulated.

SPEAKER 1: The internet is the only place where freedom of expression exists. I don't think we should make any attempt to regulate it. Any idea that is worth thinking is worth expressing.

SPEAKER 2: You say that we shouldn't regulate information on the internet because it's the only medium where freedom of expression exists. You also believe that any thought is worth expressing. I see your point, but on the other hand . . .
[Now Speaker 2 gives an opinion.]

U nit Reflection

In this unit you have learned about various barriers to effective communication. Write a contract with yourself outlining goals for improving your communication skills, three strategies that will help you achieve those goals, and how you will evaluate the effectiveness of your strategies within a given time frame.

Unit 5

The Cutting Edge

DISCUSSION

1. Leonardo Da Vinci lived in the late 15th and early 16th centuries. He was fascinated by the human and natural worlds and studied them in close detail. He was also very much a futurist. What do you find remarkable about his sketches on these pages?

2. What changes have you witnessed in science and technology over the past decade? Do you think that technology is changing at a faster rate than it did during your grandparents' generation?

3. What do you think will be the most significant advance in science or technology during your lifetime?

4. What are some of the negative aspects of technological advancements?

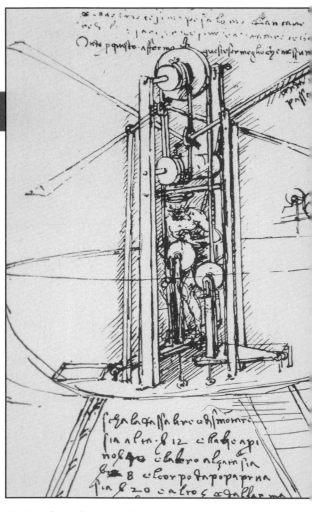

Design for a flying machine.

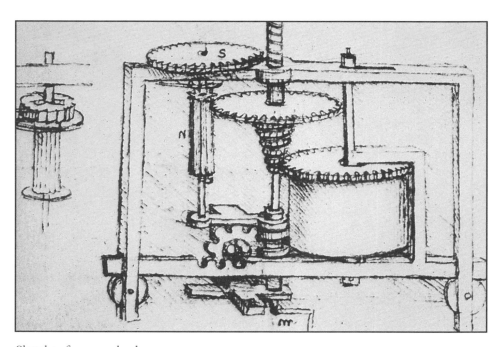

Sketches for cog wheels.

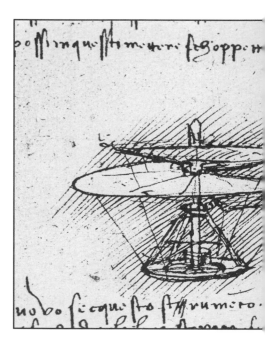

Design for a flying machine with human operator.

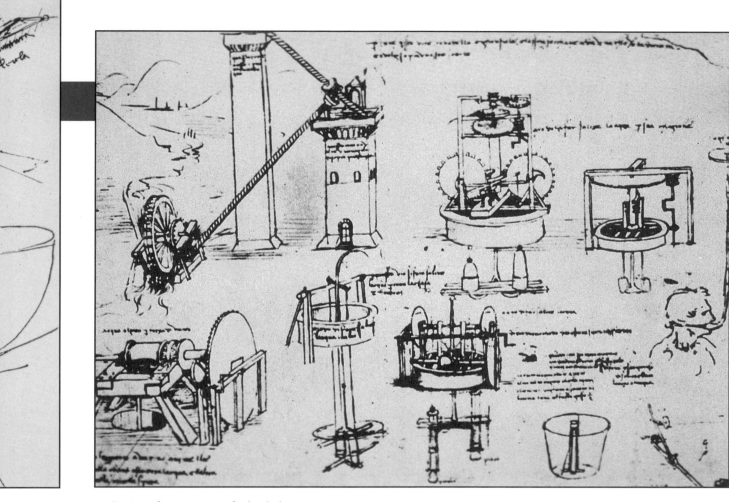

Designs for a variety of wheeled pumps.

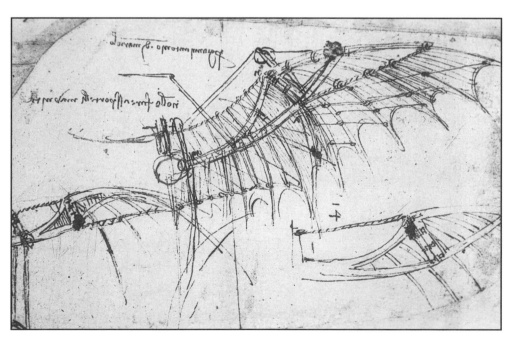

Wings for a flying machine.

Before You Read

Dr. Isaac Asimov, one of the most renowned science fiction writers of the 20th century, believed that science fiction serves a very important function in our society because it helps us to deal with the rapidly accelerating changes in science and technology we are experiencing. Science fiction discourages us from believing that things will remain as they are and encourages us to think about future changes and how they may impact on our lives. During the 1960s, for example, many people feared that advances in technology would eliminate a massive number of jobs. This fear of the unknown was allayed somewhat by scenes in *Star Trek*, arguably the best-loved science fiction series in the world. *Star Trek* showed people and machines co-existing. People were in control of machines; the machines did not control people.

Star Trek was created by Gene Roddenberry. Roddenberry hired scientists to act as consultants for the show so that the technology portrayed in the episodes would be as accurate and credible as possible. You will read an article written by Dr. David Allen Batchelor, who has a PhD in physics, entitled "The Science of *Star Trek*."

Working in teams of three or four, discuss the following questions before you read the article.

1. In what ways do you think the technology portrayed in science fiction today is a glimpse of our future reality?

2. Based on the title of the reading and the introduction above, what are two questions you expect the reading to answer?

3. Based on the title, list 10 to 15 words you are likely to find in the reading.

4. Why do you think the *Star Trek* series have such an appeal to so many people?

he Science of *Star Trek*

1 Is *Star Trek* really a science show, or just a lot of gee whiz nonsensical Sci-Fi? Could people really do the fantastic things they do on the original *Star Trek* and *Next Generation* programs, or is it all just hi-tech fantasy for people who can't face reality? Will the real world come to resemble the world of unlimited power for people to travel about the galaxy in luxurious, gigantic ships and meet exotic alien beings as equals?

2 Well, as for the science in *Star Trek*, Gene Roddenberry and the writers of the show have started with science we know and s-t-r-e-t-c-h-e-d it to fit a framework of amazing inventions that support action-filled and entertaining stories. Roddenberry knew some actual basic astronomy. He knew that spaceships unable to go faster than light would take decades to reach the stars, and that would be too boring for a one-hour show per week. So he put warp drives into the show – propulsion by distorting the space-time continuum that Einstein conceived. With warp drive the ships could reach far stars in hours or days, and the stories would fit human epic adventures, not stretch out for lifetimes. Roddenberry tried to keep the stars realistically far, yet imagine human beings with the power to reach them. Roddenberry and other writers added magic like the transporter and medical miracles and the holodeck, but they put these in as equipment, as powerful tools built by human engineers in a future of human progress. They uplifted our vision of what might be possible, and that's one reason the shows have been so popular.

3 The writers of the show are not scientists, so they do sometimes get science details wrong. For instance, there was a show in which Dr. Crusher and Mr. LaForge were forced to let all of the air escape from the part of the ship they were in, so that a fire would be extinguished. The doctor recommended holding one's breath to maintain consciousness as long as possible in the vacuum, until the air was restored. But as underwater scuba divers know, the lungs would

The starship *Enterprise* from *Star Trek: The Next Generation*.

Captain Jean-Luc Picard and Lieutenant Commander Data try to solve a problem.

rupture and very likely kill anyone who held his breath during such a large decompression. The lungs can't take that much pressure, so people can only survive in a vacuum if they *don't* try to hold their breath.

4 I could name other similar mistakes. I'm a physicist, and many of my colleagues watch *Star Trek*. A few of them imagine some hypothetical, perfectly accurate science fiction TV series, and discredit *Star Trek* because of some list of science errors or impossible events in particular episodes. This is unfair. They will watch Shakespeare without a complaint, and his plays wouldn't pass the same rigorous test. Accurate science is seldom exciting and spectacular enough to base a weekly adventure TV show upon. Generally *Star Trek* is pretty intelligently written and more faithful to science than any other science fiction series ever shown on television. *Star Trek* also attracts and excites generations of viewers about advanced science and engineering, and it's almost the only show that depicts scientists and engineers positively, as role models. So let's forgive the show for an occasional misconception in the service of an epic adventure.

5 So, what are the features of *Star Trek* that a person interested in science can enjoy without guilt, and what features rightly tick off those persnickety critics? Well, many of the star systems mentioned on the show, such as Wolf 359, really do exist. Usually, though, the writers just make them up! There have also been some beautiful special effects pictures of binary stars and solar flares which were astronomically accurate and instructive.

6 So, the bottom line is: *Star Trek* science is an entertaining combination of real science, imaginary science gathered from lots of earlier stories, and stuff the writers make up week-by-week to give each new episode novelty. The real science is an effort to be faithful to humanity's greatest achievements, and the fanciful science is the playing field for a game that expands the mind as it entertains. The *Star Trek* series are the only science fiction series crafted with such respect for real science and intelligent writing. That's why it's the only science fiction series that many scientists watch regularly . . . like me.

Comprehension Check

Find words in the reading that are synonyms for the following words or that match the following definitions.

Paragraph 1:   a) extraordinary _____

                    b) foreign _____

                    c) ridiculous _____

Paragraph 2:   d) imagined _____

                    e) changing from the natural condition _____

                    f) state of being connected without break _____

Paragraph 3:   g) put out _____

                    h) continue to live _____

                    i) replaced _____

Paragraph 4:   j) difficult _____

                    k) co-workers _____

                    l) shows (*n.*) _____

Paragraph 5:   m) consisting of two parts

                        _____

                    n) over-precise or picky about details

                        _____

Paragraph 6:   o) something interesting because never experienced before

                        _____

                    p) increases _____

                    q) not based on reality

                        _____

Reading for Information

What evidence is there in the reading for the following statements?

1. *Star Trek* promotes science and technology.

2. Roddenberry based his shows on scientific facts; however, he took some liberties with scientific details in order to accommodate the reality of television programming.

3. *Star Trek* attracts a diverse audience including well-educated people such as scientists.

4. Some of the science portrayed in the shows is not just stretched truth – it is inaccurate.

For Discussion

1. Did the reading answer the two questions your team anticipated in the "Before You Read" section?

2. What are two questions the reading answered that your team did not anticipate?

3. How important is it that the technology portrayed in science fiction shows is accurate?

One Step Beyond

1. This article was written by a man who has a PhD in physics. He has studied science at the university level for about ten years. With this fact in mind, is there anything unexpected about the vocabulary or tone used in the article?

2. Who is the intended audience for this article? What aspects of the language and sentence structure support your opinion?

Speaking

In *Star Trek* episodes, the starship *Enterprise* often visits colonies in various galaxies on peaceful missions. In teams of three or four, imagine that you are a colony the *Enterprise* visits regularly because you specialize in advanced communication technology which enables interstellar and interspecies communication. Describe your planet, the environment, your people, and the product you export. Create a commercial promoting the virtues of your product and the hospitality and services that your planet can provide for potential customers. Present your commercial to other teams.

Writing

Working in a team of three or four, create a brochure for your product. Describe the product, what it can do, and who it will benefit. Use vocabulary that will show how unique your product is.

Grammar Focus 1

NOUN CLAUSES

1. Defining Noun Clauses

A clause is a group of words that contains both a subject and a verb. Noun clauses are dependent or subordinate clauses that must be connected to independent or main clauses for meaning. There are three types of noun clauses. (Note that there is no comma between the main clause and a noun clause.)

1. Noun clauses that begin with *that*

EXAMPLE: Many futurists predict ⟨*that*⟩ *we will be travelling to other planets for our vacations in the future.*

Noun clauses beginning with *that* use statement word order: **that + subject + verb.**

In spoken English, *that* is often omitted.

EXAMPLE: I think *[that] I'll spend my fiftieth birthday on Mars.*

2. Noun clauses that begin with question words such as *who, what, when, where, why, how, how much,* etc.

EXAMPLE: No one can realistically predict ⟨*what*⟩ *life could be like on other planets.*

When a question word is used in the noun clause, the subject precedes the verb. This is statement rather than question word order.

Tip

Note that the auxiliaries *does, did,* and *do* are found in questions but not in noun clauses.

EXAMPLE: Does Carmen like *Star Trek*?
Do you know *whether Carmen likes Star Trek?*

3. Noun clauses that begin with *if /whether*

EXAMPLE: No one can guarantee ⟨*if*⟩ *species from other planets will visit us in peace.*

- *If* and *whether* are used when changing yes/no questions into statements or reporting yes/no questions.

- *If/whether* noun clauses use statement word order: **if/whether + subject + verb.**

- *If/whether* noun clauses can be used in questions or statements.

EXAMPLES: Is Data a human?
Do you know *if Data is a human?*

Will you watch *Star Trek* tonight?
I don't know *if I'll watch Star Trek tonight.*

Tip

If and *whether* can be used interchangeably, however, *whether* is considered more formal.

2. Verbs Introducing Noun Clauses

Noun clauses are often used after verbs that express thoughts, beliefs, understanding, or communication (mental activity verbs). Two examples are given below. For a more complete list of these verbs, see the Appendix on page 159.

EXAMPLES: Scientists can't <u>prove</u> *that there is life on other planets yet.*
By watching *Star Trek*, we <u>learned</u> *that Scotty was the chief engineer.*

Exercise A

1. Read the following paragraph and identify the four noun clauses.

On *Star Trek: The Next Generation*, one of the ship's officers is an android named Lieutenant Commander Data. He is a human-looking robot whose actions indicate that he has all the capabilities of a self-aware super computer; however, he lacks human emotions. At a recent conference on cybernetics, the president of the American Association for Artificial Intelligence revealed that the creation of an android like Mr. Data is the ultimate goal of his field of technology. At this point, scientists are unable to say whether it can actually be done. Watching Commander Data weekly on television allows us to imagine what it might be like if we were to co-exist with androids in the future.

2. Examine the sentences that contain the noun clauses. What function does each noun clause have in the sentence?

3. All the noun clauses in this paragraph function as _____ in the sentences and answer the question *what*?

Grammar Focus 1

Exercise B

Change each question in parentheses to a noun clause.

EXAMPLES: (What are the real costs of technological advances?)

Many people do not know *what the real costs of technological advances are.*

(Will there be enough jobs for everyone in the future?)

No one can predict *whether there will be enough jobs for everyone in the future.*

1. (Which computer should he buy?)
   John doesn't understand . . .
2. (Where will the jobs of the future be?)
   We can't imagine . . .
3. (Who is the best science fiction writer?)
   Liam asked . . .
4. (What career should they choose?)
   Many teenagers don't know . . .
5. (When will androids be possible?)
   Who knows . . .
6. (Should all students learn to use computers?)
   Schools need to decide . . .
7. (Do you like to read science fiction?)
   I would like to know . . .
8. (Is there any truth in science fiction?)
   Many people question . . .
9. (Do we need to worry about the effects of technological advances?)
   I'm not really sure . . .
10. (Will people live on Mars some day?)
    I wonder . . .

Grammar In Use

Complete the following sentences with a noun clause.

EXAMPLE: Scientists observe . . .
Scientists observe *that some of the technological equipment featured on Star Trek is not feasible in the future.*

1. The show's writers do their best to guarantee . . .
2. Not all scientists agree . . .
3. In the future scientists will announce . . .
4. Recent advances in computer technology mean . . .
5. In the next 200 years, scientists will discover . . .
6. As medical science makes new advances, many people assume . . .
7. In order to make the show work in a one-hour format, Roddenberry realized . . .
8. Many people fear . . .
9. Educators recognize . . .
10. It's not too difficult to imagine . . .

Vocabulary 1

Noun + Preposition Collocations

1. When learning new vocabulary, it is important to learn words that often go together. Use a good dictionary to find the prepositions commonly used after the following nouns. You will come across these combinations often in scientific literature.

   a) a debate _____
   b) a degree _____
   c) an argument _____
   d) an analysis _____
   e) an example _____
   f) a reputation _____
   g) an experiment _____
   h) an observation _____
   i) an article _____
   j) an investigation _____
   k) an examination _____
   l) research _____

2. Write a sentence for each noun + preposition combination.

Listening 1

T5.a

Before You Listen

In English we use various short expressions (verbal gambits) to manage our conversations (e.g., "In my opinion . . .", "Do you mean . . .?") Working in a team of two or three, fill in the following chart with expressions that you already know.

Expressions to Clarify	Expressions to Jump Into a Conversation

Expressions to Show Disagreement

Focused Listening

You will hear a conversation amongst three friends. During their lunch break, they are discussing what they did the previous evening. As you listen, put a checkmark beside any expressions you hear that you listed in your chart. Add any other expressions that you have not already listed.

For Discussion

1. What do you think the relationship is between the three people? Give examples of vocabulary and tone to support your opinion.

2. What type of audience do you think science fiction shows like *Star Trek* appeal to most? least?

3. *Star Trek* has spawned several spin-off shows and movies. Which ones are you familiar with? Describe your favourite scene or episode. If you are not a *Star Trek* fan, describe why you don't like to watch the shows and what type of shows you prefer instead.

Are androids (robots in human form) like Lieutenant Commander Data and his evil brother Lohr possible in the near future? Why might Data be one of the most popular and fascinating characters?

Reading 2

Before You Read

In teams of three or four, discuss the following.

1. How do people predict future trends?

2. What radical changes do you anticipate in technology over the next 200 years?

3. Do you think people will be living on other planets during your lifetime? What might the lifestyle on another planet be like?

4. Discuss four significant technological advances that have occurred between your grandparents' generation and your own. Choose two advances that have had positive consequences and two that have not. Discuss your choices with the other teams to determine if all teams are in agreement.

Note-Taking

You will read two excerpts from *History of the Future,* a book written by Peter Lorie and Sidd Murray–Clark that details their vision of the future. A good reading strategy for challenging material is to pause after each paragraph to reflect on its meaning and take notes. Apply this strategy. Read each paragraph in the excerpts and then write one or two sentences expressing the main idea of each paragraph in your own words.

History of the Future

Excerpt 1

We have a habit of looking at the future from inside the past. The human mind is conditioned in such a way that what is to come remains, in the majority of minds, an extension of what has gone. We base every-
5 thing on our experience – particularly in today's scientifically-oriented, "rational" scheme of life.

Much popular prediction takes the form of tracing existing trends within science and technology through to a highly mechanized and scientific future.
10 We imagine the world to be something unfolding according to our rational view of the present. And yet, it may be that there is something completely different facing us in the coming centuries.

In the early parts of the first century of the next
15 millennium, the capabilities of science will be still greater and more sophisticated – sophisticated enough to create potentially the greatest catastrophe in history.

If we consider the central theme of mankind and
20 his world as one existence, inter-connected to a complete extent, then any genetic engineering that is undertaken must inevitably alter everything around it. The old methods of mating two different breeds of animals at least allowed existence to create something
25 that failed – the power of birth was in the hands of life. But in our future, this power will be removed for the genetic scientists will be, indeed already are, creating fundamental changes in the very chemistry of life itself, bypassing any natural opportunity to
30 right the situation into the normal balance. Mankind, in the form of his scientists, will finally have found a way of doing what he has always desired to do – master nature. And in mastering nature he will effectively have mastered himself. Except that one
35 simple factor will have been forgotten – that there is no difference between the master and that which has been mastered – they are one and the same. This is therefore like taking a whip and beating one's own back with it – cutting off our nose to spite our face.

40 And it is in this vein that we shall be examining the future years – tracing the likely results of the genetic revolution and where it is going to take us. And in the same vein we will examine the likely future history of disease, for running closely along-
45 side genetic manipulation comes the very basis of why man is in such a *dis-eased* state.

The combination of going against nature and attempting to force the issues of existential life brings the major factor which causes us to create such a
50 plethora of powerful illnesses. If we are out of harmony with life, attempting always to master it, we are also out of harmony with ourselves and thus create cancer, AIDS, and all other unhappy physical ailments which currently have no solution.

55 The way forward may not be through the accepted channels of medicine but along a very different avenue indeed – possibly even through the death of medicine itself into a world which cares nothing for cure but looks deeper to the roots and the power of
60 prevention.

Excerpt 2

In the 22nd century our desire to explore and expe-rience our universe has driven us forward so that time itself becomes simply a measure of our techno-logical advances. We strive deeper and deeper in an
65 attempt to understand – not to empathize, but master. And thus we view the planet as a tool and nature a device for us to exploit and use to further our own ends. However, this lust is blinding so that we explore without seeking and experience without feeling.

70 The ability to travel into space has the possibility of changing this process in the future. Those few people in our present time who have experienced space travel have come back with a new perception of our planet Earth. Their experience has made them
75 realize that rather than being the planet's adversary they are in fact part of it. This realization has made these astronauts feel instead of being ["citizens of a particular nation"] they are "planetary citizens."

The launch of the Martian Cycler in the next
80 millennium will be the first of commercial links

How are we dealing with diseases such as cancer and AIDS? Will the focus and direction of current medical research be the same in the future?

between Earth and Mars, making it possible for the first time, for mass travel between two planets. Nick-named by its users as the Martian Metro, the Cycler will be composed of two living quarters in the shape
85 of pyramids connected by a trusswork girder joining the pyramids at their points.

The craft will travel continuously between the two planets, its six permanent crewpeople picking up and sending off passengers (up to a maximum of 52
90 passengers) at the various cyclaports along the way. From these ports the passengers are able to take taxis to the many recreational areas and resorts on route.

The future holds many mind-expanding opportunities for mankind. Only our approach to the future
95 will determine if we are able to peacefully co-exist with nature or continue to fight to master it and thus master ourselves. Our future possibilities are only bounded by our own visionary limitations.

Discuss the Vocabulary

Reading from context, discuss the meaning of the following words: *(15) millennium, (48) existential, (50) plethora, (75) adversary, (90) cyclaport.*

One Step Beyond

1. The authors' arguments are based on the premise (basic assumption) that humans see nature as an adversary to be conquered. Do you agree or disagree with this premise? Looking at global society critically, discuss examples that both support and undermine this premise.

2. The authors say that they have not based their predictions for the future on the rational development of current trends. Do you agree? Why or why not?

Writing

In teams, brainstorm responses to the following question: What recreational and resort areas can you imagine on route to Mars? Then complete one of the following writing activities.

1. Write a letter of inquiry requesting detailed information about the facilities and rates available for a Mars recreational get-away.

2. Write a detailed expository paragraph explaining one of the following.

   • the appeal of travelling to a recreational resort on Mars

   • the benefits of mass space travel

   • the impact of space travel on people's lives or attitudes

Grammar Focus 2

FUNCTIONS OF NOUN CLAUSES

As we have seen, noun clauses can function as the object of certain verbs. Noun clauses can also function in the following ways.

1. As a complement of the verb *be*

EXAMPLE: The truth is *that few people question the true value of most technological advances.*

2. As the subject of a sentence

EXAMPLE: *That computers have replaced unskilled labour* is a known fact.

3. With the subject "it" using one of the following structures:

a) it + be/seem + adjective + noun clause

EXAMPLE: It seems likely *that the jobs of the future will be in the information field.*

b) it + be/seem + a + noun + noun clause (nouns include *mercy, miracle, nuisance, pity, shame, relief, wonder, a good thing*)

EXAMPLE: It is a pity *that we can't live on the moon already.*

4. After a preposition (Note: *that* clauses cannot be used after a preposition)

EXAMPLE: The class held a debate about *what the future trends would be.*

5. After an adjective that expresses a feeling or attitude

EXAMPLE: He was alarmed *that his job was being eliminated.*

6. After a noun

EXAMPLE: The fact *that we have more information at our fingertips in a single edition of* The New York Times *today than our great grandparents learned in their whole lives* confirms that we live in the Information Age.

Exercise A

Identify the noun clauses in the following sentences and determine their functions.

1. The belief is that we will have developed the capability to live on other planets in the next 200 years.

2. I would like to enquire about whether engineers really think scientists can recreate gravity.

3. It's because of the dangers of overusing prescription drugs that many people are turning to alternative medicines.

4. It seems that people will increasingly question the value of certain medical advances in the coming century.

5. What the future will hold for our grandchildren is only speculation at this point.

6. I was amazed that the authors thought we would have recreational sites in outer space.

7. The fact that there is no gravity on other planets remains a challenge.

8. It is obvious that we are not satisfied to let nature rule.

9. Have they reached a decision on who will govern Mars?

10. Whether we will be able to live peacefully with nature remains to be seen.

Exercise B

Write new sentences with noun clauses by matching the ideas in Column A with the appropriate sentences in Column B.

EXAMPLE: I believe that space travel to Mars will be possible.

Column A

1. humankind is threatening its own existence

2. space travel to Mars will be possible

3. a cure for cancer may be found

4. many diseases are a result of human actions

5. how their research will affect our future

6. the more we know, the less we know

7. future medicine will focus on prevention

Grammar In Use

1. Write two sentences for each function of a noun clause expressing some of your ideas about future technological and scientific developments. Refer to the Appendix on page 159 and use as many of the mental activity verbs as possible in your sentences.

2. Set up a panel discussion to debate the pros and cons of advanced scientific research and its effects on our lives. To prepare, everyone should write at least one sentence on the topic which includes a noun clause. Have one person act as the moderator to ensure that everyone on the panel and in the audience has an opportunity to express his or her opinions. Use the verbal gambits you learned earlier to control the debate, to jump in, and to express your opinions.

EXAMPLE: It is a fact that even scientists are concerned about the misuse of their genetic discoveries.

Column B

a) I believe it.

b) You may be sure of this.

c) It seems possible.

d) We think so.

e) Scientists show no concern about it.

f) We know that.

g) It is a well-known fact.

Listening 2
T5.b

Before You Listen

You will hear an excerpt from a news magazine article entitled "The Dolly Debate." The writer, Bruce Wallace, exposes the latest developments in genetic manipulation as well as the controversy surrounding them.

Photographers cluster around Dolly, the world's first cloned sheep.

In teams of four or five, discuss the following.

1. Should scientists continue to experiment with manipulating gene cells?

2. What are the costs and benefits of genetic engineering?

3. Discuss controversial issues and cases in other fields of science that you are aware of. Do you think science has gone to an extreme in these cases?

4. What are the dangers involved in scientists controlling human replication?

5. The following words are used in the article you will hear. Quickly review the words and their meanings before you listen.

maxim:	principle or rule for behaviour
udder:	the bag-shaped organ of female cows, sheep, etc. that produces milk
fused:	joined
embryologist:	a scientist who studies the development of life from fertilization (of an egg, for example) to birth
convulsive:	sudden and uncontrolled
ethicists:	people who study the branch of philosophy that deals with moral principles
wacky:	strange, bizarre
to clone:	to produce an exact copy from the cells of the original when referring to forms of life
megalomaniac:	a person who has an exaggerated view of his or her own importance or power
unscrupulous:	without principles
squirming:	moving nervously

Focused Listening

Listen for answers to the following questions.

1. By what "unusual method" was Dolly created?
2. What new scientific understanding have we gained through this experiment?
3. Why might the researchers be afraid of being identified?
4. Is Dr. Alan Colman sure that his research will have no negative impact on humankind?

One Step Beyond

1. Should governments regulate scientific research?
2. Discuss the consequences of genetic engineering using the following mind map as a guide.

3. Imagine what life would be like if sexual reproduction wasn't necessary for conceiving a child and nature couldn't naturally abort embryos that should not genetically survive. How would this change our lives, our relationships, and species generation?

Vocabulary 2

A. Many scientific words in English have common roots which often originate from the Greek. With a partner, discuss the meanings of the italicized words in the following sentences. Then see if you can determine the meaning of the roots in the list below. If you need help, refer to a dictionary.

a. **bio-**	f. **cyclo-**
b. **-graph-**	g. **dyn-**
c. **patho-**	h. **poly-**
d. **astro-**	i. **geo-**
e. **auto-**	

1. a) In *biology* class we study the natural processes of living things.

   b) The doctor performed a *biopsy* to study the live cells and determine whether or not disease was present.

2. a) The nurse recorded the patient's temperature on a *graph* daily so she could quickly assess the patient's response to the treatment.

   b) The little girl asked the doctor to *autograph* her shiny white caste so she could show her friends the signature of the woman who treated her arm.

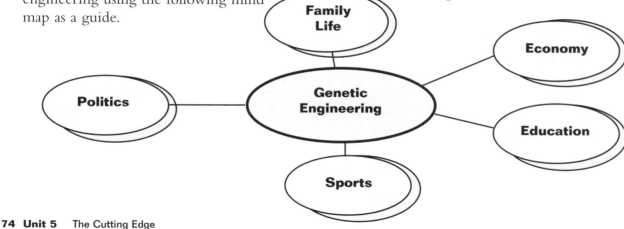

3. a) My uncle is a *pathologist* who studies diseases and how diseases affect cells.

   b) The nicotine in cigarettes is a *pathogen* because it causes cancer.

4. a) Marc Garneau was the first Canadian *astronaut* to go on a mission in space.

   b) In my *astronomy* class, we are studying the movement of the planets.

5. a) Do you enjoy reading the *autobiographies* of famous people?

   b) The pilot put the plane on *automatic* pilot when she wanted to take a short nap.

6. a) The force created by a *cyclone* can be very dangerous.

   b) A *cyclometer* measures the number of revolutions a tire makes.

7. a) They used *dynamite* to blow up the building.

   b) John is a very *dynamic* individual.

8. a) Kirin is a *polyglot* because he speaks several languages.

   b) The suspect took a *polygraph* to determine if she was telling the truth.

9. a) *Geologists* are studying lava from the latest eruption to see if they can learn more about the Earth's core.

   b) People once held the *geocentric* belief that the Earth is the centre of the universe, but it is not.

B. In teams of three, brainstorm a list of other words you know that contain these roots.

Unit Reflection

Your class is reponsible for producing the latest copy of a newsletter entitled "The Cutting Edge." Each student should submit a short article responding to the issues raised in this unit or other "cutting edge" developments in science and technology of interest. Distribute your newsletter to other classes, local libraries, and at least five friends.

Unit 6

It Stands to Reason

DISCUSSION

1. What are "brain teasers" or "mind benders?" How do they challenge us?

2. Try the puzzle below. What was the most difficult part of this activity? What strategy did you use in linking the dominoes?

3. What other types of activities can you think of that help develop our intellectual powers?

Like spotted dominoes, the picture dominoes below can be linked to form a chain. The bottom half of each domino begins a story that continues in the top half of another domino. For example, the bottom half of domino A (man frightened by shark) leads to the top of domino I (laughing kid with shark fin on back). The bottom of domino I, beginning a new story, leads to the top of . . . ? Eventually, the chain ends at the top of domino A.

A B C D E

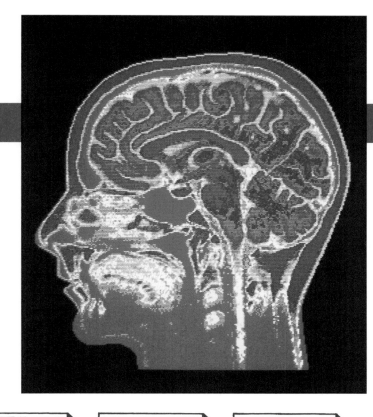

[Answer: The chain proceeds as follows: A-I-K-H-B-N-F-O-D-G-C-M-E-L-J-A.]

Vocabulary 1

Below are a number of words associated with the subject of intelligence. Fill in the blanks using the appropriate words.

deduce	reasoning	ingenuity
analogy	logic analysis	potential
rational	ignorance	wisdom
argument conclusions	spatial	riddle

1. Her _____ in this case is faulty. She clearly did not understand all the facts.

2. The comparison of the human brain to a vast computer is a common _____.

3. Despite her high IQ, the woman never realized her full _____ .

4. "What can we _____ from the facts?" asked the detective.

5. The effective problem-solver goes beyond logic to solve problems. She uses _____ .

6. His _____ of the facts of the case prevented him from solving it.

7. Einstein said, "_____ is more important than knowledge."

8. The danger of publishing scientific studies in mainstream newspapers is that people may draw false _____ .

9. Use _____ to solve this brain teaser.

10. A thorough _____ of the clues led the detective to the killer.

11. How to determine the suspect's innocence remains a _____ .

12. His speech was weakened by his unconvincing _____.

13. He made a _____ decision based on the facts.

14. This map reading activity is designed to develop your _____ reasoning.

One Step Beyond

Try this test of your word knowledge. The answer to each of the questions below is one of the 14 words in the bull's eye target. As you hit each answer, you may cross it off, since no word in the target is used more than once. When all the questions have been answered, the three unused words can be arranged to form a popular English proverb.

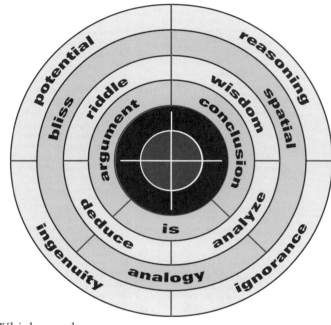

Which word:

1. has five syllables?

2. uses an *s* in British spelling, but a *z* in North American spelling?

3. without its last letter makes a word that is the opposite of *digital*?

4. is a verb that in its noun form adds *-tion*?

5. is an adjective that relates to the position of objects and the distances between them?

6. rhymes with a word that is a musical instrument popular in country music?

7. can mean the ending of a story?

8. without its third syllable means *purpose*?

9. is a noun, but adds the suffix *-ative* in its adjective form?

10. contains the following smaller words: *is, sow, do,* and *mow*?

11. can also be associated with energy in physics?

Reading 1

Before You Read

You will read an article about defining and measuring human intelligence. Before you read, try the quiz below and discuss the results.

Are You a Genius?

There's a good chance that you're more intelligent than you think you are. Our intellectual power is awesome. One popular way of testing the intellectual ability of a person is through an Intelligence Quotient (IQ) test. Try it. Feel free to use paper and pencil – a genius at work rarely does everything in his or her head. There are bonus points for finishing in less than 25 minutes.

1. While Bill was walking his dog, he met his mother-in-law's only daughter's husband's son. What relation was this person to Bill?

2. What is the missing number in this series? **1   3   9   __   __   81   243**

3. Which of the following proverbs best matches the meaning of "All that glitters is not gold?"

   a) Fine feathers make fine birds.

   b) A fool and his money are soon parted.

   c) You can't tell a book by its cover.

   d) A penny saved is a penny earned.

   e) There's a light at the end of every tunnel.

4. I met my friend the test pilot, who had just completed an around-the-world flight by balloon. With the pilot was a little girl of about two. "What's her name?" I asked my friend whom I hadn't seen in five years and who had married in that time. "Same as her mother," the pilot said. "Hello Susan," I said to the girl. How did I know her name if I never saw the wedding announcement?

5. How many blocks are in this construction?

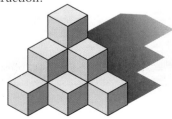

6. Here are the scrambled letters of an everyday object. Unscramble the word.

   R R R R F G I A E T E O

7. If Karen is 10, Arabella is 20, and Jim and Neal are both 5, but Richard is 10, how much is Jennifer by the same system?

8. After paying all your holiday bills, you find you have just $9.60 in your pocket. You have equal numbers of quarters, dimes, and nickels, but no other coins. How many of each of those three coins do you have?

9. Which of the following words is least like the others?
   a) house   b) palace   c) cave
   d) mansion   e) stable   f) kennel

10. How many 9's do you pass when you start at 1 and count up to 100?

11. One four-letter word will fit on all three lines below to make new words with the word preceding and the word following (example: IN D O O R STOP – Indoor and Doorstop). The same word must be used for all three lines. What's the word?

    B A C K _ _ _ _ S O M E

    F R E E _ _ _ _ M A D E

    F O R E _ _ _ _ B A G

12. Ann has the same number of sisters as she has brothers, but her brother Bill has twice as many sisters as he has brothers. How many boys and how many girls are in the family?

13. What letter would logically come next in the following series?

    J   F   M   A   M   J   ?
    a) M   b) J   c) E   d) R

14. Complete the analogy by filling in the two blanks with words from the list in parentheses. The words have the same relation as the two nouns in the first phrase: Eyelid is to eye as _____ is to _____.

    (window, glass, view, curtain, pane)

15. The following is a common proverb in disguise. Put it in its common form.

    "THOSE PERSONS WHO RESIDE IN VITREOUS CONSTRUCTIONS ARE WELL ADVISED TO REFRAIN FROM HURLING HEAVY PROJECTILES."

16. A folded triangle is shown below. Which of the lettered diagrams shows the triangle as it would look unfolded?

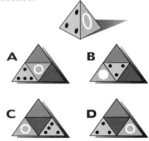

17. The spy was captured easily, and his coded message proved so simple that the lieutenant saw its importance immediately. Here it is. Uncode the message. What does it say?

    ALICE: TOM TOLD ANN CARTER KILLY AND TED, DAVID ATWOOD WAS NOT MOVING OUT NOW. DAVID AWAITING YOU.

18. All the vowels have been removed from the following remark, and the letters have been broken into groups of three. The two letters at the end are insignificant. Replace the missing vowels.

KNW LDG SPW RXX

19. A certain rule has been followed in the numerical squares below. Figure out the rule, and fill in the question mark with the correct number. (The rule applies vertically and horizontally.)

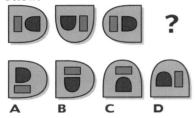

15	3	5		24	4	6
5	1	5		6	1	?
3	3	1		4	4	1

20. Which of the lettered designs best completes the sequence shown below?

To see how you scored, check the answers on page 157. Then read about scoring below.

Scoring:

Give yourself one point for each correct answer. You receive an extra five points if you finished in less than 15 minutes; three additional points if you finished in less that 20 minutes; two additional points for finishing in less than 25 minutes.

20-25 points: You are an ideal candidate for the MENSA, an international high-IQ society. Members score in the top 2% on standard intelligence tests. Members include people with advanced degrees and people who never finished high school.

15-19 points: You are among the most intelligent people around – a clear Candidate for MENSA membership.

10-14 points: A most respectable score. You might want to try taking the complete, standard MENSA test.

Below 10 points: You must have had a bad day. Even if you didn't, remember that many successful, intelligent, and creative people don't do well on tests like this.

For Discussion

1. Do you think your score on this quiz was accurate? Why or why not?

2. Based on your experience with this quiz and other tests, discuss and list some of the problems with measuring intelligence through tests such as this one.

3. How would you define "human intelligence?"

Note-Taking

As you read the article on the next page, make point-form notes of the key ideas.

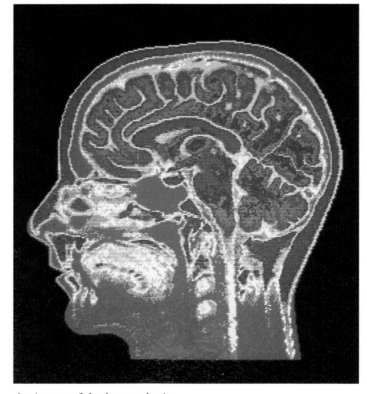

An image of the human brain.

Intelligence: The Human Miracle

What is intelligence and how can we measure it? The human ability to think has fascinated philosophers, psychologists, and educators for centuries. Measuring intelligence, however, is a relatively new science.

5 The origins of modern intelligence tests are found in the work of Alfred Binet, a French psychologist of the early 1900s, and his colleague Theophile Simon. Binet recognized that children had different levels of intelligence. At the time, children who were failing in 10 school were simply expelled. Binet believed, however, that these children should be given a thorough assessment of their intellectual abilities before being dismissed from school. He argued that children who were "intellectually retarded" should be placed in 15 special classes and be separated from those children failing school because of behavioural or emotional problems. Consequently, he and Simon designed a test that would measure a child's basic mental abilities without regard to what the child had already learned.

20 There are now several types of IQ tests. However, although adapted for North American culture at Stanford University and modified over the years, the Binet model remains a standard tool for the assessment of overall intelligence in both adults and chil-25 dren. In such tests, intelligence is measured in terms of an intelligence quotient (IQ). The following are the most commonly accepted categories of intelligence as measured on a scale similar to that of the Binet test:

IQ Range	Percentage of Population	Intelligence Category
0 - 70	3	Mentally defective
70 - 80	8	Borderline defective
80 - 90	16	Low average
90 - 110	46	Average
110 - 120	16	High average
120 - 140	10	Superior
140 - 200	1	Very superior

SOURCE: Marilyn Mach vos Savant, *OMNI I.Q. Quiz Contest* (New York: Omni Publications International, Ltd., 1985), p. 21.

30 Intelligence testing boomed in the 1930s, with schools, businesses, and the military administering them eagerly. Today, however, the subject is surrounded by much controversy. One reason for this is that while IQ scores are very successful in predicting 35 academic achievement, they are poor predictors of success later in life. Many great political and business leaders, for example, do not have high IQ scores. Another reason for the controversy is that women and some minorities consistently receive lower scores 40 on standard IQ tests than white males, suggesting that intelligence tests may be culturally and socially biased.

If intelligence tests cannot predict future success in life, what is their real value? Modern IQ tests do have 45 their place. They can tell us whether we have the intellectual abilities to succeed in graduate studies or to play chess well. They cannot, however, tell us whether we have what it takes to be successful in politics or business. And they tell us nothing about 50 our potential to be creative in music.

Most of us don't know our IQ score, although we probably have some sense of how intelligent we are. Whether or not we believe we are intelligent may be more important to our success than how intelligent 55 we actually are. Intelligence is in some ways a self-fulfilling prophecy. In other words, if we think we are intelligent, we are more likely to act that way. Unfortunately, our assessment of our own intelligence is more likely to stem from the opinion of others 60 than from an objective assessment of our own. How our parents, siblings, and spouses treat us greatly influences how intelligent we think we are.

While we might expect our teachers to provide a more objective assessment of our intelligence, expe-65 rience shows that this may not be the case. In fact, according to some experts, teachers are able to identify only about half the gifted, when left to rely on their unaided judgement. Is it any surprise then that Thomas Edison was called a dummy and subse-70 quently dropped out of school? Similarly, Albert Einstein was told by one of his teachers that he would never amount to anything and, indeed, failed high school math. When Isaac Asimov was in graduate school at Columbia, one of his professors told

75 him, "The trouble with you, Asimov, is that you can't write!"[1] Nonetheless, he remains one of the greatest science fiction writers of our time. Given these limitations, perhaps we should re-consider how we define and measure intelligence.

80 Some experts, most notably Howard Gardner, Professor of Education at Harvard University, argue that intelligence is not a single entity at all and that every human has multiple intelligences, including spatial, musical, personal, and athletic ones. In his
85 brilliant book *Frames of Mind*, Gardner defines intelligence as "the ability to solve problems, or to create products, that are valued within one or more cultural settings."[2] He goes one step further, however, to argue

that culture can actually influence the development 90 of intelligences.

The debate surrounding this subject continues. But whether we believe that humans have multiple intelligences that cannot be measured by standardized tests or that humans share a single general capacity to 95 think logically, one fact remains: human intelligence is one of life's great miracles.

1. Marilyn Mach vos Savant, *OMNI I.Q. Quiz Contest* (New York: Omni Publications International, Ltd., 1985), p. 7.
2. Howard Gardner, *Frames Of Mind: The Theory of Multiple Intelligences* (New York: Basic Books, A division of HarperCollins Publishers, Inc.), 1993.

Comprehension Check

Read each statement below and decide whether the reading supports the statement (S), refutes the statement (R), or neither supports nor refutes the statement (N).

1. ☐ Men generally do better than women on IQ tests.

2. ☐ An IQ test can predict how successful someone will be as a business leader.

3. ☐ Minorities generally receive lower scores on IQ tests because they are disadvantaged in learning.

4. ☐ Teachers are the most objective assessors of a person's intelligence.

5. ☐ People who have low IQ scores usually have exceptional abilities in music or math.

6. ☐ According to commonly accepted categories of intelligence, as many people are below average intelligence as are above average intelligence.

Main Ideas

Share the notes you made of the main ideas with a partner. Have you included any unnecessary details? Have you included all necessary details?

One Step Beyond

1. What are the two opposing definitions of intelligence discussed in this reading?

2. The reading states that traditional IQ tests may be biased towards the white male. What implications might this have for our society?

Writing

Write a summary of the reading "Intelligence: The Human Miracle."

Speaking

When debating an issue, it is important to use examples, facts, anecdotes, and statistics to support your arguments. Choose one of the following statements and argue in support of or against it.

● Identifying and labelling students in school as "gifted" (highly intelligent) does more harm than good.

● Human intelligence cannot really be measured.

● Intelligence is the key to success.

Grammar Focus 1

IF STATEMENTS (CONDITIONALS)

One grammatical structure that is often used when drawing conclusions and making deductions is the "*if . . . , then . . .*" statement. *If/then* statements express a dependent relationship. If a certain condition is true, then a specific result will also be true.

condition

EXAMPLE: If Mary didn't arrive until 5:00 p.m., *(then) she couldn't have met Mr. Smith at the party. He left at 4:30 p.m.*

result

In this sentence, if the condition is true, then the result will be true; the result depends on the condition. In this sense, *if* acts as a subordinate conjunction that joins a dependent clause to an independent clause and shows a condition/result relationship. (Note that the word *then* is optional.)

We can distinguish two main kinds of structures with *if*:

1. Real Situations – *if* with "ordinary" tenses
2. Unreal Situations – *if* with "special" tenses

1. Real Situations (if with "ordinary" tenses)

Real *if* sentences express real or possible situations that can happen in the past, present, or future. These sentences therefore use ordinary tenses with *if*: present tense to refer to present time or unspecified time, past tense to refer to past time, and so on. In other words, we use the same tenses as with other conjunctions.

PRESENT (NO SPECIFIC TIME): If you constantly *criticize* children, they *develop* low self-esteem.

PAST: If the student *took* the test in early May, (then) she *received* her results by June.

Note, however, that a real *if* sentence uses the simple present in the *if* clause even when the situation refers to the future.

FUTURE: If you *test* the child, (then) you *will discover* that he is gifted.

(not: if you will test the child . . .)

If you *don't complete* your assignments, (then) you *will have wasted* your time taking this course.

The structure is: If + subject + verb . . ., (then) subject + verb . . .

Exercise A

Complete the sentences.

1. . . . , you are in the superior intelligence category.
2. If you are in the low average intelligence category, . . .
3. If a student was failing in France at the turn of the century, . . .
4. . . . , you will have missed an interesting book about human intelligence.
5. If we believe that we are intelligent, . . .

2. Unreal Situations (if with "special" tenses)

When we want to express that a condition is unreal – unlikely to happen, imaginary, or impossible at the time of speaking – we use special tenses to "distance" our language from reality. To express the idea that the condition is unreal, we use some form of the past tense in the *if* clause and *would (or might, could)* + verb in the result clause.

EXAMPLE: If her IQ were* 200, she would be in the top 1% of the population. (However, it isn't likely that her IQ is 200, so she isn't in the top 1%).

* Although it is most correct to use *were* in the first and third person singular form of the verb *be* in expressing unreal conditions, *was* is becoming more common in both speaking and writing.

a) Unreal conditions in the present and future

To show that a condition is unlikely or impossible now or in the future, we use a past tense in the *if* clause (even though the meaning is in present or future), and *would + verb* in the result clause.

EXAMPLE: If I *knew* the answer, I *would* tell you. (but I don't know the answer)

The structure is: If + subject + verb (past tense) . . ., (then) subject + would + verb

Grammar Focus 1

Tip

In conditional clauses, the difference between, for example, "if I *pass* the test" and "if I *passed* the test" is not a difference of time. Both sentences can refer to the present or future; the past tense suggests that the condition is less likely to happen, impossible, or imaginary.

b) Unreal conditions in the past

To show that a past condition did not happen, we use a past perfect tense (*had + past participle*) in the *if* clause, and *would have + past participle* in the result clause.

EXAMPLE: If you *had asked* me, I *would (might, could) have told* you.

If you *had finished* high school, you *would have gotten* a better job.

Tip

An *if* clause can come at the beginning or end of a sentence. When an *if* clause comes at the beginning, it is separated by a comma. Compare:

If you believe you are intelligent, you are more likely to behave intelligently.

You are more likely to behave intelligently if you believe you are intelligent.

Exercise B

There are ten sentence parts below. Some express causes and some results. Rebuild the sentences by matching causes with results and insert *if* at the appropriate point.

1. we wouldn't be motivated to set our standards high

2. IQ tests predicted success in life

3. he wouldn't have become one of the greatest science fiction writers of our time

4. women and minorities didn't consistently score lower on IQ tests

5. we knew our IQ was low

6. they would be used more readily

7. Asimov's professor had been accurate saying Asimov couldn't write

8. we judged people's value to society based on their IQ

9. the efforts of many great people would go unnoticed

10. perhaps we wouldn't question the social and cultural biases of the tests

Grammar In Use

Victoria Sanchez has always wanted to work in law. She wants to apply to a reputable law school. She needs very high marks to be accepted and although she has the minimum average she needs, she's afraid it might not be high enough. Many other students have a higher average than hers. She does have very valuable experience, having volunteered in a law office for the past two years. She has also been very active in politics in her community and she is president of the student council at her university. She wonders if she should wait another year, take some more courses, and try to raise her average. Her uncle, who is a reputable lawyer himself, knows someone at the law school and although she wants to succeed on her own, she wonders if she should ask her uncle to "pull some strings." Victoria has acquired a handsome debt through her student loans, which she is anxious to pay off. If she can avoid drawing out the process, she'd prefer to get into law school now and get her studies over with. She's not sure what to do.

In teams, help Victoria to make a sound decision.

1. List at least five of Victoria's options in this situation (some are mentioned above, but there may be others.) Discuss the consequences of each option.

2. Advise Victoria as to what course of action she should take.

T6.a

MARGARET THATCHER:
"Let me give you my vision."

JOHN F. KENNEDY: "Ask not what your country can do for you, but what you can do for your country."

MARTIN LUTHER KING JR.:
"I have a dream."

CHARLES DE GAULLE:
"The flame of French resistance."
(1940)

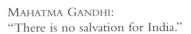

NELSON MANDELA:
"Our march to freedom is irreversible."

MAHATMA GANDHI:
"There is no salvation for India."

WINSTON CHURCHILL: "I have nothing to offer but blood, toil, tears, and sweat." (1940)

Before You Listen

In teams of three or four, complete the following questions.

1. The pictures on the previous page show a number of political leaders who were known as effective speakers. Identify the leaders you know and discuss who they were.

2. Think of some great political or social leaders from your native culture. Discuss who these leaders are and why you consider them great. Do you also consider them intelligent?

3. Think of speeches you have heard that have left a lasting impression on you. Discuss, in detail, what makes a good speech.

4. You will hear a speech by a great American leader of the 1960s. Discuss what you know about the political and social environment of the United States at that time. Include a discussion of the following terms: Civil Rights Movement, Ku Klux Klan, the Supreme Court, the Constitution.

5. The following words are used in the speech you will hear. Quickly review the words and their meanings before you listen.

segregated: separated from another group

humiliated: treated in a way that makes one lose self-respect

oppression: ruling people in a harsh way by taking away their freedom to protest (complain)

justice: what is right and fair

intimidation: a threat or threats made to persuade people to act against their wishes

coercion: intimidation

bitter: to have feelings of anger especially because of something considered unfair

with dignity: in a way that deserves respect because of self-controlled behaviour

abyss: a deep hole that appears to have no bottom

perpetuation: continuation

despair: hopelessness

Listening

Read the introduction below. Then listen to the speech and answer the following questions.

Martin Luther King, Jr. (1929-1968), a black American Baptist pastor, was the right man in the right place at a moment when history demanded a man of stature to become the leader of his people. That moment occurred in 1955, when King led the victorious campaign against segregated seating in buses in Montgomery, Alabama. Never before in American history had a black leader succeeded in a prolonged attack upon oppression. King subsequently led the Civil Rights Movement, insisting like Mahatma Gandhi had in India, on non-violence.

About a thousand black Americans packed Holt Street Baptist Church on the night of 5 December 1955, the day when the first campaign started. Outside, another 5000, mainly labourers and servants, listened to the speeches over the loudspeaker.

As King and Ralph Abernathy entered the church together, all heads turned. As the audience applauded and television cameras began to shoot from all sides, the crowd grew quiet. Then King, speaking without notes or a manuscript, delivered the speech that first drew him to national attention. (He was 26 years old.) You will hear excerpts from that speech.

Comprehension Check

1. What feelings are you left with after listening to this speech? What adjectives would you use to describe the speech?

2. What is the central message of this speech? That is, what is Dr. King asking the people to do? Why is he asking them to do this?

Focused Listening

Listen to the speech again in segments. First read the questions below for each segment, then listen for the answers.

a) *First Segment* Dr. King creates a sense of unity in his audience by discussing two things they all have in common. What are those two things?

b) *Second Segment* The title of the speech is "There comes a time when people get tired." What are the people tired of?

c) *Third Segment* Dr. King asks his people to act. What does he ask them to do?

d) *Fourth Segment* In this segment, Dr. King compares the protests of organizations such as the Ku Klux Klan with the protests of blacks. Complete the chart below.

	White Citizens' Councils/ Ku Klux Klan	Black Community of Dr. King
The group's goal		
The group's methods		

e) *Fifth Segment* Dr. King is trying to convince his audience that what he is asking them to do is "right." What comparisons does he make to convince the listeners of this?

f) *Sixth Segment* In this final segment, Dr. King asks his people to behave in a certain way throughout their struggle. What two contrasting behaviours does he encourage?

One Step Beyond

Read the transcript of this speech on page 158. The language of formal speeches is quite different from that of everyday conversation. Not only are the words more formal, but the phrases are often very poetic or literary. Using language this way adds to the impact a speech can make on its audience. Martin Luther King, Jr. uses a number of these poetic phrases to create strong images in the listener's mind.

Read the sentences or phrases below and discuss what images they create. Then discuss what they mean and re-write them in simpler, less formal English.

1. "We are here also because of our deep-seated belief that democracy transformed from thin paper to thick action is the greatest form of government on Earth."

2. "We are . . . tired of being kicked about by the brutal feet of oppression."

3. ". . . people get tired of being pushed out of the glimmering sunlight of last July and left standing amid the piercing chill of an Alpine November."

4. "Let your conscience be your guide."

5. "If we fail to do this, our protest will end up as a meaningless drama on the stage of history."

6. "Its memory will be shrouded with the ugly garments of shame."

7. "There lived a great people – a black people – who injected new meaning and dignity into the veins of civilization."

On April 4, 1968, Dr. King was assassinated by a sniper on the balcony of his second-floor room at the Lorraine Motel in Memphis. James Earl Ray, his killer, was later captured and convicted of the murder.

Dr. King won the Nobel Peace Prize in 1964.

Writing

1. "Each time a man stands up for an ideal, or acts to improve the lot of others, or strikes out against injustice, he sends forth a tiny ripple of hope and crossing each from a million different centres of energy and daring, those ripples build a current that can sweep down the mightiest walls of oppression and resistance."

This quotation is taken from a famous speech by US Senator Robert Kennedy in 1966. Write a paragraph explaining the meaning of this quotation.

2. Write a biography of a famous historical figure that you admire.

Speaking

Choose one of the titles below and write a short, formal speech. Use powerful words and expressions, and persuasive arguments. Present your speech to the class.

- The causes and effects of racism
- Leadership – innate or developed?
- Why we need heros
- The power of words
- What makes a great leader?

Reading 2

The ultimate test of your deductive powers just might be the solving of a cunning crime. Detectives and sleuths such as Sherlock Holmes and Hercule Poirot have captured the attention of millions of readers precisely because of our fascination with analyzing clues and solving mysteries. The success of board games such as *Clue*, as well as a host of weekly television mystery and detective shows, proves that we love to test our ability to draw conclusions from facts and observations. Use your reasoning powers to solve the mystery in the following reading "Who Murdered Ellington Breese?"

Before You Read

A murder has been committed. Look at the crime scene in the illustration. Imagine that you are the servant who found the body and describe the scene to a detective.

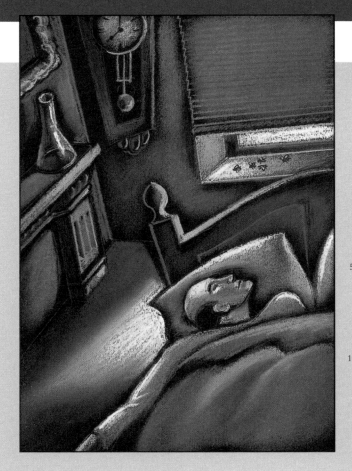

Who Murdered Ellington Breese?

Suspicion of guilt of the murder is narrowed down to two men. Which of them committed the crime and how do you know? Examine carefully the following established facts, then answer the questions following the reading.

London was shocked on the morning of June 5, 1925, by the news of the murder of a distinguished citizen. Ellington Breese, founder and president of the Breese Chemical Works, near Gravesend, had been murdered
5 by poison gas generated in his bedroom during the night.

Breese was a good deal of a "character," and insisted on living not far from his works, in what had been a Victorian gentleman's country house near the river.
10 The police investigation revealed the following pertinent facts:

Breese had been found dead in his bed at eight o'clock in the morning by his servant, who for years had aroused him at that hour. On the mantelpiece

15 (there was no fireplace) the police found a glass flask of about one quart capacity. Its stopper was missing. It was the kind of glass vessel familiar to any chemical labora-tory. Experts said that one chemical poured upon another would have generated the poison gas immedi-
20 ately, and that diffusion in the room must have followed quickly. Neither on the glass flask nor on other objects were fingerprints found.

Although both windows had been up eight inches [20 cm] from the bottom, the practically instantaneous effects
25 of the gas had killed every living thing in the bedroom. Breese's pet bullfinch lay dead in its cage. Half a dozen flies lay dead on the window sills. It was exceptionally hot weather and the flies had been troublesome. The dark green blinds at the windows were found drawn
30 down nearly to the bottom of the lower window sash, dimming the murder chamber, though the sun shone brightly outside.

The wavering finger of suspicion began to point with equal emphasis at two young men, each of whom
35 was connected with Ellington Breese's business and had had enough laboratory experience to have manu-factured the deadly gas.

Breese Walters, nephew and only surviving relative of the murdered man, was one suspect. Adam
40 Boardman, Breese's confidential secretary, was the other. Each protested his innocence, each to a degree had an alibi. According to the police investigations, so far as could be determined, both had good records, no debts or entanglements. Both seemed deeply affected by the
45 tragedy.

Neither man seemed capable of committing such a cowardly crime. Yet the police reflected upon the terms of Breese's will, which divided half his estate — about one hundred thousand pounds — between the favourite
50 nephew and the devoted employee. The other half of the estate Breese had bequeathed to charity. The terms of the will, drawn five years before, had never been a secret.

Walters and Boardman had maintained cordial but
55 not close relations while in the employ of Breese. Each expressed confidence in the innocence of the other.

The coroner examined the body at 9:30 a.m. and declared that Breese had been dead at least four hours, and possibly for as long as ten hours. The position of the
60 body in the bed indicated to a certainty that death had overtaken Breese while in his bed, to which he had been confined by a slight illness. The police, cherishing a uniform suspicion of Walters and Boardman, decided that they would know the murderer when they knew
65 approximately the hour in which the poison gas was generated in Breese's bedroom.

Boardman, the secretary, had been with Breese until a little after 11:30 p.m. He admitted it, and his leaving the house about a quarter to twelve was confirmed by
70 the testimony of old Mrs. Grew, Breese's boyhood nurse and housekeeper, whose room was near Breese's on the second floor. Boardman had been discussing business matters with his employer, who was laid up in bed con-valescing from influenza. He admitted returning to
75 Breese's bedroom for a moment after first leaving it, in order, he said, to secure a briefcase which he had for-gotten. At that time, he said, he put out the bedroom light at Breese's request, and closed the door upon leaving. And after leaving Breese's home, Boardman
80 went in his little two-seater car straight to the Dormy House of a local golf club, where he lived. Through the rest of the night and until the body was found his alibi was perfect.

Walters had been in Manchester all day. He got back
85 to London in time for a late supper at his club, and arrived at the house near Gravesend at one o'clock in the morning. Mrs. Grew heard him enter, came out and spoke to him on the second floor landing and asked if there was anything she might do. Walters said he was
90 not hungry and would go straight to bed. He asked about his uncle's health, heard that Boardman had been there until nearly midnight attending to details of business, and observed that his uncle must be recover-ing nicely from his influenza if he could remain at work
95 so late. He went upstairs to his room on the third floor.

Mrs. Grew, who was suffering from rheumatism, returned to her room on the second floor, read for a while, and then went to sleep — not until 2:30 a.m., she believed. From that time until the discovery of the
100 murder, Walters' claim of innocence, like Boardman's, had no support from other testimony than his own.

In short, the police suspected, and their suspicions proved well founded, that if Breese died before mid-night it was Boardman who liberated the gas that killed
105 him; and that if Breese died after midnight, then Walters was the slayer of his uncle.

You have now all the evidence from which Scotland Yard shrewdly fixed the approximate time of the crime and thereby the identity of the murderer.

(14) *mantelpiece:* a shelf above a fireplace

(15) *glass flask:* glass jar commonly used in a
         chemistry laboratory

(16) *stopper:* lid, top

(20) *diffusion:* spreading

(31) *chamber:* room

(39) *suspect:* a person who is considered possibly
         guilty

(42) *alibi:* a claim that a suspect was somewhere else
         when the crime took place

(44) *entanglements:* relationships that border on the
         illegal

(48) *will:* legal document that states who will receive
         the dead person's money and possessions

(48) *estate:* possessions and money

(51) *to bequeath:* to leave to someone after your
         death

(51) *charity:* organizations that do good social work
         and are not in the business of making
         money

(54) *cordial:* friendly and polite

(57) *coroner:* an official (often a doctor) who investigates
         any suspicious deaths

(74) *influenza:* flu

Comprehension Check

A. Get the facts.

1. Before solving the murder, you must be sure of the facts in the case. Complete the chart below.

Victim's name: _____

Victim's occupation: _____

Place, date, and time of the murder: _____

_____

Person who found the body: _____

_____

Where and when the body was found: _____

_____

How the victim died: _____

Murder weapon: _____

B. Now that you have the facts, consider your suspects.

2. Who are the suspects in this case?

3. What possible motives might each have for killing Ellington Breese?

4. Does each suspect have an alibi? What is it?

C. The next step is to take a closer look at possible clues.

5. a) In point-form, describe the crime scene in detail.

    b) Are there any clues at the crime scene that might be significant in solving this crime? If so, highlight them.

D. Now make some deductions based on the clues.

6. According to the police, what do you need to determine to discover which suspect committed the murder?

7. What clues can help you to determine this? (HINT: Consider the crime scene.)

E. One Step Beyond – Finally, solve the crime.

8. Who killed Ellington Breese?

9. How did you deduce this?

[Answer on page 157.]

Grammar Focus 2

MODALS

Modals, such as *should, could, must, will,* etc., are words that give additional meaning to a verb. The meanings of modals vary with the context. When we express deductions and conclusions, for example, we often use the following modals: *must/have to, could, might, can't/couldn't, should* (expectation).

1. Expressing Degrees of Certainty

When we draw conclusions or make deductions, we do so with varying degrees of certainty. The thermometer below shows which modals are used to express different degrees of certainty.

No	Degree (Approximate)	Yes
certain +	100%	The butler killed him. (statement of fact)
	95%	The butler *must have* killed him. (statement of deduction)
	75%	The butler *could have* killed him.
The butler *might not have* killed him.	50%	The butler *might have* killed him.
I don't think that the butler killed him.	75%	
	95%	
The butler *couldn't/can't have* killed him. (impossibility)	100%	certain −
The butler didn't kill him. (statement of fact)		

Note: Adding the negative form (*not*) to the modal changes its meaning altogether. For example, *couldn't/can't* means impossible (100%), but *could* means possible (about 75%).

Exercise A

Rewrite the statements below using a modal to show the indicated degree of certainty.

1. The victim has four brothers. (*95% certain*)
2. The coroner didn't determine the exact time of death. (*impossibility*)
3. The murderer was not a family member. (*50% based on deduction*)
4. She didn't see him walking into the library. (*impossibility*)
5. The maid saw the murderer. (*75% certain*)

2. Modals of Deduction, Expectation, and Possibility

The following modals are most often used to express deductions, expectations, and degrees of possibility.

Function	Modals	Examples
A. Deduction	have to, must	The murder *must have occurred* after ten o'clock. Mr. Flame, the secretary, *has to know* who telephoned. After all, Mr. Flame answered the phone.
	can't, couldn't (impossibility)	His wife *couldn't have committed* the murder. She was in New York at the time.
		The wife *can't have known* that her husband was at the pub, because he hadn't planned to go there.
B. Expectation	should (based on logic)	The police were called half an hour ago. They *should be* here shortly. After all, we aren't that far from the police station.
C. Possibility	could (strong possibility)	It *could have been* either the nephew or the secretary; both had a motive.
	might, may (weak possibility)	The victim *might not have known* his killer, but I suspect that he did. After all, there was no sign of a struggle.

Grammar Focus 2

Modals are never used without the verbs they modify. They act in a similar way to verbs, but they are not independent verbs.

modal + verb

PRESENT: He *must be* out for a walk.

modal (not) + verb

She *couldn't be* at home. She's vacationing in Cuba.

In the past forms, modals are followed by *have + past participle (pp)* of the verb.

modal + have + pp

PAST: She *could have been* at home. She wasn't in school that day.

modal (not) + have + pp

The victim's wife *couldn't have known* about the weapon.

Because we cannot make deductions about future facts, modals of deduction cannot be expressed in future time. Similarly, we do not use modals of deduction in question form. We can, however, use modals of possibility and expectation in these forms.

Exercise B

Read the facts. What can you conclude or expect? Use modals in your answers.

1. A letter from Belgium takes about five days to arrive in Canada. Mr. Van Riet sent a letter to his granddaughter about seven days ago.

2. Nicholas and Christopher have been practising their piano duet for two months in preparation for the music festival today.

3. Mrs. Humphreys was told that Pia and Iris live in Zurich.

When the girls arrive in Canada on a school exchange and stay with Mrs. Humphreys, she is surprised to hear them speaking German. She expected them to speak French.

4. Jennifer lives in New Brunswick. She is accused of stealing her neighbour's rubber hose.
   The hose was stolen last Saturday.
   Jennifer was in Montreal last weekend.

5. An airplane crashes on the border between Canada and the United States.
   The survivors are buried in Canada.

6. A man married his widow's sister.

Grammar In Use

Using expressions of probability and cause/result relationships, work in teams to solve this riddle as quickly as possible. The first team to solve the puzzle must explain the solution to the rest of the class.

Miss White, Miss Black, and Miss Gray are out for a stroll together. One is dressed in white, one in black, and one in gray. "Isn't it odd," says Miss Gray, "that our dresses match our last names, but no one of us is wearing a dress that matches her own name?" "So what?" said the lady in black. Which lady is wearing which dress? [Answer on page 157.]

Vocabulary 2

In English, verbs are often combined with adverbs and prepositions. In some cases, these combinations are quite easy to understand, for example, *kneel down* (verb + adverb) and *walk on* (verb + preposition). However, in some combinations the verb in the phrase does not have its usual meaning. In the sentence "He *carried out* an investigation", the verb in the phrase *carried out* doesn't have the same meaning

as in "He *carried* his grocery bag to the car." When a verb combines with an adverb or a preposition to create a new meaning, it is called a *phrasal verb*.

1. The human mind is capable of making sense out of what appears to be senseless. The words in the following sentences have been arranged in alphabetical order. Each sentence contains a phrasal verb. Put the words in the correct order, identify the phrasal verb, and guess its meaning. [HINT: Look for words that form logical phrases first, then put the phrases in order.]

a) a abilities. focus intellectual IQ measuring on person's tests

b) couldn't figure how logic out puzzle. solve teacher The the to

c) able account for his not on performance poor student test. The the to was

d) a education education equitable is ministry more system. The towards working

e) a about bring Dr. free hard King Luther Martin of prejudice. society to worked

f) and any between find graduate if infant intelligence. out psychology relationship student stimulation The to there wanted was

2. Write a synonym for each of the phrasal verbs.

3. Write a sentence using each of the phrasal verbs.

peaking

Problem-Solving Process

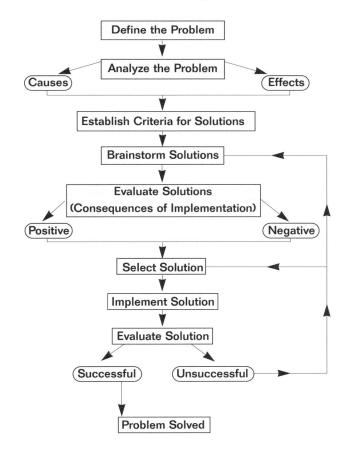

1. Discuss the problem-solving process shown in the flow chart.

2. Use this problem-solving process to solve one of the problems below. Stop after the "Select Solution" step.

a) One university is becoming very concerned about academic dishonesty. Students have been caught lying, cheating, plagiarizing, and engaging in other types of dishonest academic conduct. You are a member of a university-appointed team of students whose job is to solve the problem.

b) Town officials have become alarmed at the increase in gang violence in the community. According to the politicians, the number of gang-related crimes and violence has increased five-fold over the past year. The community has been suffering an economic depression since its major employer, a local factory, shut down its operation two years ago. Many families left the town for brighter prospects elsewhere. School enrolment is down and the high school drop-out rate has also increased. You are a volunteer member of a committee of concerned citizens who are meeting to solve the problem.

nit Reflection

In teams, discuss the meaning of the expression used as the title for this unit: "It stands to reason." Use this example to help you.

If many great political and business leaders do not have high IQs, it stands to reason that measuring IQ is not useful for predicting success in the political and business arenas. List one or two synonymous expressions for "It stands to reason."

Unit 7

All the Rage

DISCUSSION

1. The photos show some popular North American fads of the 20th century. Match the pictures with the appropriate captions below.

   Motoring – "A Rich Man's Toy" (1900s-1910s)
   The Mah-Jong Craze (1920s)
   Gangster Movie Madness (1930s)
   Swooning over Sinatra (1940s)
   The Car Cramming Craze (1950s)
   The Funky Look (1960s)
   Disco Fever – John Travolta (1970s)
   Nintendo™ Fever (1980s)
   The X-Files Craze (1990s)

2. Discuss which of these fads you are familiar with and why they were so popular.

3. What do you think "popular culture" means?

Reading 1

Before You Read

Working in teams of four or five, complete the following activities.

1. Describe some current fads amongst these age groups: 10 to 12-year-olds, 14 to 16-year-olds, 18 to 25-year-olds, and 35 to 40-year-olds. Think of hit movies, music bands, recreational activities, and so on. List at least five.

2. Discuss why people are attracted to these fads.

Reading

You will read an essay about popular culture fads in the 20th century. An essay is made up of three parts: (1) an introductory paragraph, (2) several developmental paragraphs (the body), and (3) a concluding paragraph. Each part has a particular function. The writer of the following essay "This Craz(e)y Century," wrote two introductions and two conclusions, then couldn't decide which introduction and conclusion worked best. Read the body of the essay first, then choose which introduction and which conclusion (on pages 98 and 99) you think fits best. Be prepared to give your reasons.

> TRIVIA *In the late 1950s a bizarre fad that involved packing as many people as possible into a small space such as a car or telephone booth swept through college campuses across the continent. In one instance, seven students held their breath long enough to cram into a phone booth that was immersed in a swimming pool.*

This Craz(e)y Century

Leisure time as we know it today is a relatively new concept. One hundred and fifty years ago, the average work week in North America was 70 hours. When people weren't working, they were . . . well, working.
5 The "good ol' days" were not necessarily happy ones. Men and women worked hard on the farms, in the town factories, and at home – and children did the same. By the 1920s, however, some 35 million North Americans were going to the movies at least once a
10 week. When did this metamorphosis take place? The new technologies around the turn of the century were pivotal in taking us from a society of workers to one of players.

No other technological advancement was more
15 important to our leisure time than the automobile. At first, the automobile aroused widespread resentment as "rich folk" casually ran down livestock on their way to their favourite shore resorts and spas. In the cities, millionaires such as Alfred Gwynne Vanderbilt
20 terrorized pedestrians by touring their cars through the city streets at reckless speeds of more than 10 miles an hour [16 km/h]. Some owners flaunted their wealth by adorning their cars with gold-plated lamps and jewelled emblems. There was no doubt
25 about it, the car was "the rich man's toy." Nonetheless, this object of resentment soon became a symbol of success, and car manufacturers like Oldsmobile quickly began to appeal to the pride of the newly affluent. Touring became a favourite pas-
30 time, as did racing. The North American love affair with the automobile, which persisted throughout the following decades, was perhaps not so much a love affair with the technology of cars as it was a love affair with the freedom they brought. As more people
35 began to own cars, new crazes and manias exploded on the pop culture scene with the same fervour, particularly as the advertising and entertainment industries grew.

The hottest entertainer to hit the music scene in
40 the 1940s, for example, was a five-foot-ten [175 cm], 135-pound [61 kg], blue-eyed singer from New Jersey. Frenzied bobbysoxers across the continent

squealed and swooned over this frail-looking youth. Known as "The King of Swoon," Francis Albert
45 Sinatra had a voice that thrilled millions. His success as a male teen-idol was mystifying at a time when the North American image of manliness was a brawny soldier in combat fatigues. Psychologists explained Sinatra's lure in various ways from "mass
50 frustrated love" at a time when most men were away at war or just returning, to "an urge to feed the hungry," referring to his scrawny build. Interestingly, Sinatra's frail and innocent appearance masked a rather rugged, fist-fighting youth who once threatened to
55 break the nose of a news photographer attempting to photograph him with Ava Gardner, then Hollywood's reigning *femme fatale*. Sinatra's most famous hits included "White Christmas," "Fools Rush In," and "Night and Day." He was immensely
60 popular. Thousands of girls skipped school to attend his concerts, and some ardent fans dug up his footprints when it snowed and preserved them in the refrigerator. Sinatra fever caused such a ruckus in North America that, according to the *New York*
65 *Herald Tribune*, Congress affirmed that "The Lone Ranger and Frank Sinatra are the prime instigators of juvenile delinquency in America." But by the start of the new decade, the fire of "Frankie mania" had smouldered to a faint glow – that's how crazes go, in
70 one minute and out the next.

Of all the crazes, perhaps the fashion fads are the quickest to come and go. In the 1920s it was bathing suits – striped full-body suits which covered the thighs and often the shoulders. Yet of all the fashion
75 fads in the 20th century, perhaps none was as out-landish as the funky look of the sixties. A funky outfit wasn't something you could buy at a store. Rather, teens created a funky ensemble by putting together styles, colours, and jewellery that didn't
80 follow the rules of "*haute couture.*" Instead of wearing a shirt, for example, a teen might wear a red-fringed vest and multi-coloured beaded necklace. A pair of pants could be laced from pieces of leather strips. The more bizarre the look, the funkier it was.
85 The revolutionary fashion of the sixties mirrored the anti-establishment psyche of the decade's young.

TOP: Frank Sinatra – the voice that thrilled millions in the 1940s
BOTTOM: Bathing suit fashion in the 1920s – a passing fad

Along with drugs, sexual freedoms, acid rock, and the "love-in," the funky look was a reaction to the confining values and conservatism of the previous
90 decades. But those who dreamed of a non-materialistic society that focused on the collective would have their dreams shattered in the decades to follow.

Technology again set the trends of our leisure activities in the "me decade" of the 1980s with the
95 introduction of cable television and video games. By 1989 cable television was found in 60% of all homes with television sets, giving viewers more choices in channels. Sales of VCRs were at 465 000 at the beginning of the decade. Rentals of movies on video
100 became so popular that by 1985 income from video rentals for home viewing equalled the income studios made from movies shown in theatres. Video games were played in 20% of all American homes. In fact, in the second half of the 1980s Nintendo™ games were
105 so popular that they hurt the sales of traditional toys. The instant success of cable and video technology may have been due in part to the developing trend of "cocooning," a word coined by Faith Popcorn in her famous *Popcorn Report* to describe the habit of staying
110 at home to protect ourselves from the big, bad, ugly world outside. Our desire to tune in each week persisted throughout the eighties into the nineties with hot new shows and oldie revivals, which mirrored the evolving culture of the time.

---

(10) *metamorphosis*: change from one form to another
(17) *livestock*: farm animals such as cows and sheep
(22) *flaunted*: showed publicly
(29) *affluent*: rich
(36) *fervour*: excitement
(42) *bobbysoxer*: a popular name for teenage girls of the 1940s and 1950s when many wore bobby socks (short socks covering the ankles)
(43) *swooned*: were emotionally affected, almost to the point of fainting
(43) *frail*: weak
(57) *femme fatale*: an attractive, mysterious woman who leads you to danger
(61) *ardent*: eager, passionate
(67) *juvenile delinquency*: youth crime
(69) *smouldered*: burned slowly without a flame
(75) *outlandish*: strange

Introduction 1

As a new century dawns and we struggle to redefine our society within a changing social, political, economic, and spiritual framework, it is both comforting and relevant to take a nostalgic look at North American pop culture in the 20th century. After all, it is popular culture that defines our collective psyche and perhaps even shapes who we are to become. Parading through the fads and manias that have won our affections since the turn of the century offers us insight into the century's opportunities, struggles, victories, and defeats. It also reminds us that we engage in these nonsensical, but nevertheless fun pastimes in our continuous efforts to overcome the humdrum of our daily struggles.

collective psyche: psychological characteristics of a group

Introduction 2

Would you swallow a live goldfish. . . or two. . . or three? Well, in the 1930s goldfish swallowing swept the continent as one of the hottest crazes on campuses across North America. A little "cuckoo" you think? Perhaps, but when you consider some of the more bizarre fads to hit North America over the past century, it seems that embracing the outlandish has been more popular than watching the six o'clock news. Fads are by their very nature popular yet short-lived pursuits. Social trends, on the other hand, are general changes in the way people behave in society. Most people confuse the two, thinking they are the same. By examining some of the trends and fads North Americans have embraced over the last century, we will begin to understand the fundamental differences between the two.

Conclusion 1

Is it a coincidence then that at the end of the millennium, when North Americans mistrust their governments more than ever before, the hottest television series centres on political conspiracy? With an audience of 40 million viewers, *The X-Files*, a series about two FBI agents investigating paranormal activity, has grown from a minor cult hit into a huge mainstream success. How long *The X-Files* craze will last no one can say. But, like all crazes and fads, this one appeals to our social psyche. It is uncertain to what extent, if any, popular culture shapes our values. What is certain, however, is that popular culture *reflects* our values - our collective fears and hopes (and in the case of *The X-Files*, our political paranoia and desire to believe in powers beyond our own). Understanding the psyche of the times, a perceptive social observer could conceivably design products and services that appeal to the masses, creating a new fad. A risky venture? Perhaps, but one worth possibly millions.

Conclusion 2

Our everchanging social trends have been recorded to serve as a reminder of where we have been and where we might be headed in the future. With a new millennium crashing in on us at warp speed, we seem to be experiencing considerable social angst about what lies ahead. Journeying through the pop culture of the century, to be sure, gives us insight into our triumphs and failures — political, economic, social, and spiritual — but, more than that, it allows us to re-live a bit of our personal and collective histories. Perhaps by holding on, just a little, to the certainty of our past, we will be better able to embrace the uncertainty of our future.

TRIVIA *The Asian game of mah-jong — sort of a combination of dice and dominoes, played with tiles made from the shinbones of calves — was a ladies' club fad in America from 1922 to 1925. The American mania for the game, which peaked in 1923, soon caused a shortage of calf shinbones in China. The game was even outselling radios. Interestingly, the decline in popularity of mah-jong may be attributed to the crossword puzzle, a fad that swept America in 1924.*

Comprehension Check

1. What important development marked the change from a society where people worked most of the time to one where people enjoyed more leisure time?

2. Why did many people resent cars at first?

3. What was Sinatra's appeal?

4. What is the meaning of "anti-establishment" in the fourth paragraph?

5. Why was cable and video technology so successful in the 1980s?

6. What was the impact of video games on the children's entertainment market in the late 1980s?

One Step Beyond

1. What is the significance of the (e) in the title "This Craz(e)y Century?"

2. Because fads are interests or behaviours that are very popular for a short time, they are associated with strong emotions and high energy. List some of the words and expressions the writer uses to create a "feeling" of energy and emotion.

Writing

Based on your discussion about which is the best introductory and concluding paragraph for the essay, list the important characteristics of an effective introduction and conclusion. Then complete one of the writing activities below.

1. Write about a fad in your native country and discuss how that fad reflects the social psyche.

2. Write a review of a hit movie or television episode.

3. Write an essay explaining how the pop culture of a society affects how the rest of the world views that society.

Vocabulary 1

1. Below are some picture and letter clues to the pronunciation of words often used in the context of popular culture. Work with a partner to discover the words.

Clues: + = add the letter(s) or illustration that follows

  − = take away the letter(s) or illustration that follows

EXAMPLE: 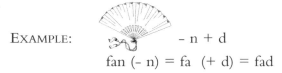 − n + d

fan (− n) = fa (+ d) = fad

a) m +  − c + ia = _____

b) two words: 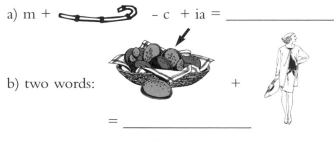 +

  = _____

c)  + = _____

d) + con = _____

e) tr + = _____

f) − ft + − l

  = _____

g)  − p + v + ⬆ − p

  = _____

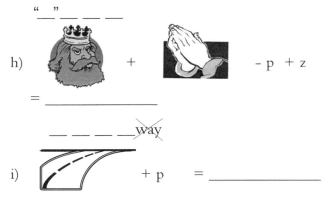

h) + − p + z

  = _____

i) + p = _____

2. Now match the words you deciphered with their meanings below and then write a sentence for each word.

EXAMPLE: f a d

  (*informal*) something that is very popular for a short period of time

  In the late 1980s Teenage Mutant Ninja Turtles™ were a fad. Today they're not even sold any more.

1) ◯ a trick or device used to attract attention

2) ◯ an extreme or abnormally high enthusiasm for a person, thing, or group, e.g., In the 1960s, crowds surrounded the Beatles wherever they went. People screamed and fainted. It was Beatle_____ .

3) ◯ a person who is admired and looked up to as an example

4) ◯ a person who is greatly loved, admired, or respected and almost worshipped like a god

5) ◯ to make something sound very important or exciting, exaggerating its good qualities

6) ◯ an observable development or change in a situation

7) ◯ a very famous person or thing that represents a set of beliefs or a way of life

8) ◯ an enthusiastic but often brief interest in something shared by many people, e.g., The car ____ began with the development of the first Model T Ford.

3. Circle the word that does not belong in each group below and give a reason for your choice.

a) mania craze fad gimmick

b) icon hype idol role model

peaking

In teams, create a new product that you believe will be the next craze. Analyze the current social climate, target your market, design your product, and develop a television commercial persuading your audience to buy the product. Be prepared to role-play your commercial.

Grammar Focus

TO + BASE VERBALS

1. Defining Verbals

Every English sentence has two main parts: a subject and a predicate. Each predicate begins with a verb which must have a tense. The verb tense tells the time period of the sentence.

subject

EXAMPLE: Studying the popular culture of a society *offers* insight into the values of its people.

predicate

Verbs, however, can also be used in other positions in the sentence where they don't have a tense. When a verb is used without a tense, it is called a *verbal*. A verbal can be used alone, or more commonly, as part of a phrase.

subject *predicate*

EXAMPLE: *Break-dancing* was a means *to express* individuality in the 1980s.

In this case, *break-dancing* and *to express* are verb forms without tense and therefore are considered verbals.

Verbals allow us to *name* activities, situations, or events almost like nouns. Verbals take three forms:

1. *To + base* (infinitive)

2. *Base + ing* (gerunds or present participles)

3. *Base + d/t/n* (past participles or passive participles)

In this unit you will learn about the first kind, the *to + base* verbals also known as infinitives. Infinitive verbals often suggest a future or expected activity. They usually indicate purpose.

Exercise A

Identify the nine *to + base* verbals in the paragraph below.

Feeling stressed is a fact of life for most people and while this may appear to be a problem of our modern times, stress has been around for longer than we realize. Many people are surprised to learn that only 150 years ago the normal work week was 70 hours – very stressful. While it is difficult to avoid stress altogether, it is possible to reduce or manage stress. There are several things we can do to manage the stress caused by our daily obligations. First and foremost, we need to balance the routines of work, family, and school with the enjoyment of our leisure time. Exercise is very effective in relieving stress. However, experts also advise us to participate in fun, sometimes nonsensical activities such as dancing, going to the movies, or simply watching television to relieve stress. This may be why so many people have eagerly embraced such silly fads as car cramming, goldfish swallowing, and collecting pet rocks. Many people participate in the latest craze simply to reduce some of the pressures of daily life.

Grammar Focus

2. Sentence Positions of *To* + *Base* Verbals

Although there are many uses of the infinitive, we will focus on six of the more common uses, based on sentence position. *To* + *base* verbals are found in the following sentence positions:

a) in an adverbial position answering the question *why?* (explaining the reason for an action)

EXAMPLE: The rock star *secretly left the concert hall by the back door* (*to avoid*) the crowds.

Here the verbal *to avoid* explains why the subject (*the rock star*) engages in the action (*secretly left the concert hall by the back door*).

> **Tip**
> Because the infinitive states the purpose of the action, *to* could be replaced with *in order to*.

b) in an object position after certain verbs answering the question *what?*

EXAMPLE: The fan *attempted* (*to get*) the star's autograph.

In such cases, the verbal acts like a noun. Some verbs require an infinitive object; others require a gerund (*base* + *ing* verbal) object. With some verbs an infinitive or gerund can be used. For a list of common verbs that are followed by infinitive objects, see the Appendix on page 159.

Some verbs require or can be followed by a pronoun, noun, or noun phrase before the infinitive.

EXAMPLE: The children *persuaded their parents* (*to buy*) the new toy.

In this example, the noun phrase *their parents* follows the verb and comes before the infinitive *to buy*.

Verbs that can take a noun or pronoun before the infinitive include:

advise*	force*	persuade*	ask	expect
remind*	beg	intend	choose	show (pronoun/noun phrase) how
need	order*	encourage*	want	tell (pronoun/noun phrase) how

* these verbs must be followed by a pronoun, noun, or noun phrase in the active voice

c) in the complement position after the verb *be* or other linking verbs where the verbal states purpose, ability, or wish

EXAMPLE: The important thing *is* (*to maintain*) a balance between work and leisure activities.

The infinitive in this example expresses a purpose.

d) as the subject of a sentence, often where "it" is placed in the subject position and the verbal is placed after the adjective or noun

EXAMPLE: (*To make*) a good low budget film is difficult.

or

It is difficult (*to make*) a good, low budget film.

In these examples, the verbal phrase *to make a good low budget film* acts as the subject. The structure with "it" is useful for emphasizing an important point because the reader's attention is drawn to the subject at the end of the sentence. The usual pattern in this structure is **it** + **be** + **adjective** + **infinitive**, but it can also be **it** + **be** + **noun** + **infinitive** as in "It is a mistake to think that fads will last."

> **Tip**
> Not all infinitives at the beginning of a sentence are subjects.
>
> EXAMPLE: (*To truly enjoy*) the plays of Shakespeare, you must see them performed.
>
> Here the verbal phrase *to truly enjoy* acts as an adverbial phrase and has the meaning of *in order to enjoy . . . .*

e) after certain adjectives where the verbal is not the subject

This is common when talking about feelings.

EXAMPLE: The fans were *happy* (*to see*) their favourite rock star.

Common adjectives that can be followed by infinitives include:

afraid	anxious	difficult
eager	foolish	fortunate
glad	good	happy
important	lucky	normal
ready	surprised	

f) in the position of post-modifier after a noun

We can use an infinitive after a noun where it states the purpose of the noun.

EXAMPLE: He brought along a *bag* (*to keep*) his books in.

We can also use an infinitive after some abstract nouns.

EXAMPLE: People have a strong *need* (*to belong*) to a group.

Some nouns in this pattern include:

ability	agreement	attempt
chance	decision	desire
need	plan	effort
opportunity	time	

Exercise B

Fill in the blanks.

1. It was nice _____ that song again.

2. It's a _____ to think that popular culture isn't important.

3. They went to the video store _____ the latest James Bond film.

4. The idea was to persuade teens _____the product.

5. The band _____ to release a new album by the end of this year.

6. The children begged _____ to buy the latest Nintendo™ system.

7. It's _____ to study the fads that were popular in the early 1900s.

8. The company made a _____ to market the new toy to parents directly instead of to children.

Exercise C

Write sentences using *to* + *base* verbals for the sets of key words below. You may use any form of the key words and add words to your sentence, but do not change the order of the key words.

1. company / advertising / appeal / teenagers
2. teachers / games / educate / children
3. parents / television / babysit / children
4. teens / like / go / clubs
5. difficult / predict / trends
6. books / discover / history
7. fashion advertisers / models / sell / clothes
8. not be / old / enjoy / classical music
9. library / sign out / bestseller
10. not easy / learn / play / mah-jong

Grammar In Use

A "Way Cool" Holiday

Work in pairs. You and your partner work at a travel agency. Four clients come to you asking for help in planning a fantasy holiday – the latest travel craze. These clients know each other because they all attend the same "Phobia Anonymous" therapy group. Each client wants to participate in as many activities as possible as long as the activity doesn't relate to his or her phobia. Plan appropriate activities for each client using the ad on the next page for the Way Cool Resort. Then answer the questions.

Clients	Phobias
Jocelyn Boutelier	heights, running
Tanja Pelikan	water, heights
Ilse Weidlich	balls, boats
Stefan Rinderman	loud noises, grass

Way Cool Resort!

The Hottest Vacation Spot on the Planet! Escape the boredom of the real world and treat yourself to a fantasy vacation at our fantastic *Way Cool Resort and Spa*. Plan to soar over crashing waterfalls and lush green islands in a private helicopter tour and dance your way into someone's heart at "The Rad," the hottest nightclub south of the equator. Call now to book your vacation or see your travel agent.

1-800-WAY-COOL

FACILITIES:

golf course   pool

private white sand beach

tennis courts   four-star restaurant

"The Rad" live entertainment club

private airport (tours)   marina

1. What would each client be afraid to do?
2. What activities might each client plan to do?
3. What facilities would each client visit? For what purpose would the client visit that facility?
5. What would each client refuse to do?
6. Where would all clients agree to go?

---

*L*istening 1

T7.a

Before You Listen

In teams, discuss the following questions. Then read the introduction below.

1. Look at the photo on the left and discuss what it might represent.

2. Have you ever heard of James Bond 007? If yes, what do you know about him? In point form, write as much information as you can about him.

3. Have you ever seen a James Bond movie? If yes, discuss it with your team members.

4. What is a secret agent?

In 1953 a lucky British public first glimpsed 007 standing alone by a roulette wheel (where else?) amid the elegant baroque of the casino at Royale-les-Eaux, observing the enemy. From the opening pages of *Casino Royale* [the first Bond novel], 007 had it all: the sophistication we envied, the danger we dreamed of, the girls we desired, the life we wanted. By the time [author Ian] Fleming died in 1964, he'd created in 14 books a mythological hero, one of the greats of the century, for Bond is part Sherlock Holmes, part Indiana Jones. Though the Bond films will probably go on forever and a series of book-sequels have already gone on too long, let us look back at the original: the British secret agent licensed not only to kill but virtually to print money. How, after all this time and over 60 million copies sold, do Ian Fleming's novels measure up? Can an outdated book-Bond ever hope to withstand an up-to-date film-Bond? James Bond novels and films were a great hit in the 1960s. Eric Ambler, arguably the finest thriller writer of all, once said that he thought the Bond books "definitely deserve to be read as literature."

Who is James Bond? A civil servant, probably born 1924; entered the employ of the Ministry of Defence at age 17, went to work for the Secret Service (MI6) after the war. He performs his duties, according to M [his boss], "with outstanding bravery and distinction" though "with a streak of the fool-hardy." He likes his eggs boiled for precisely three-and-a-third minutes, and definitely smokes too much, a blend of Balkan and Turkish tobaccos custom-made for him. (At three packs a day, they must crowd his suitcase on long assignments.) He stands a little over six feet [183 cm], weighs about 167 pounds [76 kg]; he lives in a comfortable flat in a square off the King's Road in Chelsea, London, on an income (mid-1950s) of about $4200 a year. He has few friends. He is emphatically not a spy: his job never involves stealing state secrets, blueprints for weapons, plans of invasion, etc. He is a secret agent, a loaded gun sent out to enact the will of his government without being caught.

You will hear an excerpt from *Live and Let Die*, Fleming's second James Bond novel published in England in 1954.

TRIVIA *Gangster movies came into vogue in 1927 and continued to be popular in the 1930s. More than 60 gangster movies were made between 1930 and 1935, including the fabulous* Public Enemy *starring Jimmy Cagney. In fact, the image of American gangster culture is so popular around the world that when Euro Disney was being planned, the French wanted Main Street to recreate the gangster mob era of the 1920s complete with mobsters wearing Fedoras and double-breasted suits, and wielding tommy guns and snub nose .38s. Disney, thinking it undignified, graciously refused.*

Comprehension Check

1. Where does the story begin?
2. Which main characters are introduced in this excerpt?
3. Summarize what happens.

Focused Listening

Read the questions below and then listen to the excerpt again to find the correct answers.

1. Where does Halloran lead Bond once he approaches the secret agent?
   a) into a room marked PRIVATE
   b) towards a door marked US Health Service
   c) towards a black Buick
   d) beyond the Health Service building towards the Customs office

2. In the limousine Bond turns to Halloran and says, "Well, that's certainly one of the reddest carpets I've ever seen." What does he mean?
   a) it was unusual to have a red carpet in the limousine
   b) he hadn't expected to be treated so well
   c) he was referring to Communist spies at the airport who were dressed in red
   d) he saw a large billboard advertising of his hotel with a red carpet at the door

3. Where is Bond?
   a) Washington
   b) New York
   c) Los Angeles
   d) Moscow

4. What did Bond see across the street from the hotel as he was saying goodbye to Halloran?
   a) Captain Dexter
   b) his hotel
   c) a black sedan Chevrolet
   d) a chauffeur opening the limousine door for a negress★

5. What does Captain Dexter ask Bond to do when he enters the hotel?
   a) to go straight to the check-in counter
   b) to keep his hat on

c) to go straight to the elevator

d) to take his luggage

6. In what room or on what floor of the St. Regis hotel would Bond stay?

a) the first floor

b) room 2003

c) the top floor

d) the 24th floor

7. What was unusual about what Bond saw?

a) an accident almost occurred

b) the limousine was from Harlem

c) the chauffeur was a negress★

d) a giant was sitting in the back seat of the limousine

★ Note: the terms "negress" and "negro" are no longer commonly used and may be considered offensive because of their associations with slavery (the terms were, however, common in the 1950s and 1960s when Ian Fleming wrote his books). Black or African American/African Canadian are the more common and preferred terms today.

One Step Beyond

In teams or with a partner, answer these questions.

1. The title of this chapter is "The Red Carpet." Why do you think the author gave it this title? Give the chapter another appropriate title.

2. Bond is treated royally. What facts in the recording support this statement?

3. Read the excerpt below. Then answer the questions.

Bond turned to say goodbye to Halloran and thank him. For a moment Halloran had his back to him as he said something about Bond's luggage to the commissionaire. Bond looked past him across 55th Street. His eyes narrowed. A black sedan, a Chevrolet, was pulling sharply out into the thick traffic, right in front of a Checker cab that braked hard, its driver banging his fist down on the horn and holding it there. The sedan kept going, just caught the tail of the green light, and disappeared north up Fifth Avenue.

It was a smart, decisive bit of driving, but what startled Bond was that it had been a negress [African American woman] at the wheel, and through the rear window he had caught a glimpse of the single passenger – a huge face which had turned slowly towards him

and looked directly back at him, Bond was sure of it, as the car accelerated towards the Avenue.

a) Which sentences in this excerpt create a sense of suspense?

b) What verbs, adjectives, and adverbs does the author use to heighten the suspense?

4. What is your impression of Halloran? If you had to cast an actor in this role, how would he look and why?

5. What role do you think the man, whom Bond sees in the car, will have in the story?

Writing

What happens next? The excerpt you heard covers only the first part of chapter one. The chapter continues with Bond meeting Felix, an old friend and colleague with whom Bond had worked on a previous case in *Casino Royale* (Fleming's first novel). In Bond's hotel room, Felix explains the scope of his new case to Bond over lunch. Using your imagination and without explaining the details of the case, write a one-page description of what happens following the excerpt you heard. Include a detailed description of the hotel room, the meeting of the two men, and the meal they enjoy. Write in a style suitable to a James Bond story.

Reading 2

Before You Read

The Simpsons, which premiered in 1990, is a phenomenally successful comedy television series. In fact, it is the longest-running prime-time animated show in North American television history. The popularity of *The Simpsons*, however, goes far beyond national borders – the large number of international Simpsons internet sites is evidence of this – making it a worldwide American pop culture mega success. As with other pop culture fads, the popularity of *The Simpsons* will eventually die. But future generations who look back on North American popular culture in this decade will gain insight into the social fabric of

American and Canadian family life through this dysfunctional family we love so much. Work in teams to profile the Simpsons by completing the activities below.

1. Discuss whether *The Simpsons* is popular in your native country and make a list of countries where *The Simpsons* television show is known.

2. List as many of the characters in the television show as you can and discuss their relationship to each other.

3. Discuss why you think the Simpson family is so popular.

Now read the article below by Victoria A. Rebeck and then write a summary. This article is an editorial that expresses the author's viewpoint on the popular television show.

ecognizing Ourselves in the Simpsons

The merchandising of his image on T-shirts and stickers has made his face unavoidable, even to those who don't watch the television show: Bart Simpson of the cartoon family the Simpsons has become wildly
5 popular.

Youth apparently love him and his hapless family, though the show seems meant more for adults, who constitute a large portion of its enthusiastic followers.

Drawn by cartoonist Matt Groening, author of
10 "Life in Hell," a strip that appears mainly in the alternative press, *The Simpsons* first appeared as a brief feature of *The Tracy Ullman Show* comedy series. Audience appreciation turned the awkward clan into America's favourite dysfunctional family and earned
15 them a weekly series of their own.

This is no vapid, pristine family show, however. School principals in Ohio, California, and Kentucky have condemned the show, singling out Bart as a poor role model and complaining about T-shirts that
20 feature Bart and such slogans as "Underachiever and Proud of It." Bart is a smart-mouthed, mischievous, bristle-headed boy who has two sisters: high-achiever Lisa, whose prissiness hides her talent for playing blues saxophone, and Maggie, a shapeless bag of a
25 baby who quietly observes the household misadventures while sucking audibly on her omnipresent pacifier. Heading the family are Homer, a boor of the Fred Flintstone variety, and Marge, a scratchy-voiced, well-intentioned yet ineffectual mother who sports a
30 towering teased-up hairdo.

Groening's art is childishly crude; the characters are given only a few identifying characteristics.

The Simpsons are a typical North American family – typical in a way most family-based shows never
35 acknowledge. Instead of presenting as normal some childhood traumas that most of us never face and then resolving them with presumptuous, simplistic parental advice, the Simpson children wrestle with problems like peer pressure and their own lack of
40 self-understanding while getting sincere but useless – perhaps even damaging – advice from their parents.

On one episode Lisa was feeling alienated from her peers. Growing impatient with her daughter's depression, Marge advises her that "it's not what you
45 feel inside that counts, it's how you look on the outside. That's what my mother taught me." (And isn't that what our mothers told us?) "Just push those feelings down deep inside you and smile," she continues.

"And boys will like you, you will be invited to parties and happiness will follow."

Lisa takes her mother's advice and ends up allowing other children, especially the disturbed opportunists, to take advantage of her hunger for approval. Noticing this, Marge rescinds her instructions and instead encourages Lisa's interest in blues music, which provides her a creative medium of expression for her normal feelings.

Simplistic religion is exposed when Marge drags the family to church to "get a little goodness into them." In Sunday school the children learn about heaven and hell and some of the fanciful mythos propping up this doctrine. Groening cleverly reveals how children, who tend to be literalists, can discern the folly of taking such concepts literally.

"Will my dog, Fluffy, go to heaven?" one child asks.

"No," responds the teacher to the obviously disappointed youngsters.

"How about my cat?" asks another.

"No, heaven is only for people."

Bart perceives some faulty reasoning. "What if my leg gets gangrene and has to be amputated?" he poses. "Will it be waiting in heaven for me?"

The teacher has to pause only briefly before answering authoritatively, "Yes."

"What about a robot with a human brain?" Bart presses.

The teacher rubs her head in frustration. "I don't know! Is a little blind faith too much to ask for?!"

The educators who have decried *The Simpsons* are like this Sunday school teacher: they have missed the point. *The Simpsons* is satire. Rather than engage in the pretentious misrepresentation of family life that one finds in the "model family" shows, this program admits that most parents aren't perfect. They haven't worked out their own childhood confusion, and they don't have the answers to all their children's problems. The obnoxiousness of the Simpson children and their schoolmates is their way of coping with adults who can't possibly always do right; after all, adults are only human.

Bart Simpson T-shirts do not plant ideas in children's heads. The need to rebel is part of their psyche. School principals concerned about the need for positive role models should concentrate on providing those role models, not on proscribing clothing or attacking a clever piece of satire.

The Simpsons are not the ideal family. But they are not intended to be. They provide catharsis. By laughing with Bart we take vicarious revenge on adult authority figures who emotionally abused us when we were children. And at times we laugh at Bart, who reminds us of rude youngsters we've had to endure. The Simpsons are not telling people how to act. If anything, they are giving people an outlet so they won't have to act out. The Simpsons show us in a rather bald as well as witty way what it was about our upbringing that made us brats as kids and neurotic as adults.

---

(10) *alternative press:* newspapers and magazines that are not aimed at the masses (the majority of people) and often express particular or alternative views

(16) *vapid:* boring, unimaginative

(16) *pristine:* unspoilt, perfect

(23) *prissiness:* behaving in a way that is perceived as too correct

(27) *boor:* a rude, inconsiderate person

(37) *presumptuous:* too confident and showing a lack of respect for others

(54) *rescinds:* takes back

(62) *doctrine:* a set of beliefs or a theory

(63) *literalists:* people who interpret ideas according to the exact meaning of words

(71) *amputated:* cut off

(95) *proscribing:* forbidding

(98) *catharsis:* a way to release strong emotions

(99) *vicarious:* experienced by observing the activities of other people

---

Comprehension Check

1. Why have some school principals condemned the show?

2. How does the writer describe Homer Simpson?

3. How does the writer describe Marge Simpson?

4. What advice did Marge give Lisa in one episode when Lisa was feeling alienated from her peers? What was the result of this advice?

5. How did Groening show the folly of taking religious doctrines literally in one episode?

One Step Beyond

1. The writer claims that the Simpsons are a typical North American family. What evidence does she give to support this? Do you agree or disagree?

2. How is *The Simpsons* television show cathartic?

3. How can families use *The Simpsons* television show to deal with some of the difficulties of family life?

Vocabulary 2

The mah-jong mania of the mid-1920s came to an end with the start of a new craze – crossword puzzles. Complete the crossword puzzle to the right, which includes words from the reading "Recognizing Ourselves in the Simpsons." Then design your own crossword, making up sentences for each of the words.

dysfunctional	condemn
omnipresent	trauma
opportunist	folly
pretentious	obnoxious
cope	outlet

Down

1. annoying and offensive

2. strongly exaggerated importance

3. way to release energy or emotions

4. not working the way it should

5. to deal with successfully

6. shock

Writing

Using as many vocabulary words as you can from this unit, complete one or more of the following writing activities.

1. Write an episode for *The Simpsons* which includes a lesson from daily life.

2. Write a comparison essay about "real" families versus Hollywood families.

3. Write an essay analyzing the popularity of a current television series.

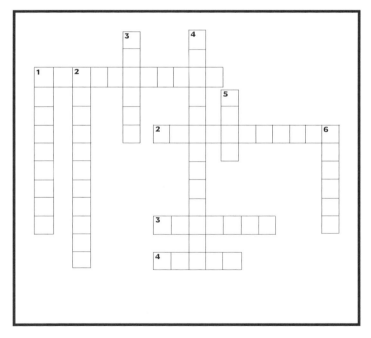

Across

1. a person who takes advantage of every chance for personal success without regard for how his or her behaviour may affect others

2. being everywhere at the same time

3. to disapprove of or criticize strongly, usually for moral reasons

4. foolishness

Listening 2

Before You Listen

1. Looking back over the century, discuss how musical styles can define a time period.

2. Identify some current hit songs and discuss why they are so popular.

3. You will hear a song about a famous fictitious American super hero, Superman. Discuss what you know about Superman and his life. What attributes make Superman a hero?

Focused Listening

Listen to "Superman's Song" by the popular Canadian band Crash Test Dummies from their *The Ghosts That Haunt Me* CD. Then answer the questions below.

1. The vocalist compares Superman to what other famous fictitious character?

2. What comparisons does the singer make between them?

3. A song's chorus, because it is repeated, contains the main message of a song. What is the main message of this song?

One Step Beyond

1. What might the jungle and the city symbolize in this song?

2. Superman has permeated North American popular culture since 1938, appearing in comics, films and on radio, TV, and Broadway. Why do you think he has remained so popular throughout the decades?

3. Popular culture has traditionally been viewed as light-hearted, nonsensical, and unimportant. Does this song support or refute this idea? How?

TRIVIA *The 1980s witnessed the transformation of an ancient sport of strength and agility into a show business arena, featuring 300 pound-plus (136 kg-plus), muscle-bound behemoths as the unlikely stars and profitable pop culture icons. Pro wrestling became one of North America's most popular sports. Its practitioners, once unable to earn a living from the game, suddenly were commanding six-figure incomes. André the Giant, Rowdy Roddy Piper, Ravishing Rick Rude, and Sergeant Slaughter became heroes to millions of kids, though the limelight in the eighties was stolen by Hulk Hogan, aka "the Hulkster".*

Speaking

In teams, create a super-hero character to share with your classmates. Include the following:

- *Personal Data:* give your hero a name, an identity, and a history
- *Description*: describe your hero's appearance, character traits, and special powers. You may wish to include an illustration.
- *Guiding Principles*: list the moral principles that guide the actions of your hero
- *Action Narrative*: create a story in which your character demonstrates heroic behaviour. You may wish to write your story, create a cartoon, do a radio play, act out the story, or simply tell your story.

Unit Reflection

This unit is titled "All the Rage." Discuss the meaning of the word *rage* and list some synonyms. How does this word relate to the fads and manias of popular culture? Based on what you have learned, choose a new title for this unit.

Unit 8

It's How You Play the Game

DISCUSSION

1. What are the advantages of physical activity to our overall well-being?
2. What types of physical activities are suitable for toddlers, teens, adults, and seniors?
3. Are there any negatives associated with sports? Do these differ between amateur and professional sports?
4. To cut costs, schools should eliminate extra-curricular sports programs. Do you agree or disagree?

Reading 1

You will read three extracts from books about popular sports and the impact of sports on culture.

Before You Read

Divide into three teams. Your instructor will assign one of the three readings to your team. Before you read, discuss the following.

1. What role do sports play in North American culture and in your culture?
2. What are some of the physical and emotional benefits of participating in individual and team sports?
3. What is a sports fanatic? Describe someone you know who is a sports fanatic.

Jigsaw Reading

Individually, read your assigned passage and then discuss the following questions with your team.

1. How do sports help build a sense of community?
2. The passage describes a certain degree of sports fanaticism. Give examples.
3. What descriptive words, phrases, and comparisons does the writer use to make the reader understand the importance of the game?

Form new teams by joining with another student from each group. You should now be in multiple teams of three. With your new teammates, take turns each briefly summarizing your passage and the response to the discussion questions.

Extract 1

The following passage is from a novel entitled *Shoeless Joe* by W. P. Kinsella. The book is about a man who feels an unexplained need to build a baseball field on his farm where former baseball stars who are no longer living can come and play. The movie *A Field of Dreams* was based on this book.

Shoeless Joe

"There's someone on your lawn," Annie says to me, staring out into the orange-tinted dusk. "I can't see him clearly, but I can tell someone is there." She was quite right, at least about it being *my* lawn, although
5 it is not in the strictest sense of the word a lawn; it is a *left field*.

Annie peeks through the drapes. "There is a man out there; I can see his silhouette. He's wearing a baseball uniform, an old-fashioned one."
10 "It's Shoeless Joe Jackson," I say. My heart sounds like someone flicking a balloon with his index finger.

"Is he the Jackson on TV? The one you yell 'Drop it, Jackson' at?"

Annie's sense of baseball history is not highly
15 developed.

"No, that's Reggie. This is Shoeless Joe Jackson. He hasn't played major-league baseball since 1920."

"Well, Ray, aren't you going to go out and chase him off your lawn or something?"
20 Yes. What am I going to do? I wish someone else understood. Perhaps my daughter will. She has an evil grin and bewitching eyes and loves to climb into

Extract 2

This passage is from *Home Game*, written by Ken Dryden, a well-known and respected hockey player, writer, and educator. The co-author is Roy MacGregor.

my lap and watch television baseball with me. There is a magic about her.

25 As I step out onto the verandah, I can hear the steady drone of the crowd, like bees humming on a white afternoon, and the voices of the vendors, like cows cawing.

"The ground is soft as a child's breath," I say to the 30 moonlight. On the porch wall I find the switch, and the single battery of floodlights I have erected behind the left-field fence sputters to life. "I've tended it like I would my own baby. It has been powdered and lotioned and loved. It is ready."

35 Moonlight butters the whole Iowa night. Clover and corn smells are thick as syrup. I experience a tingling like the tiniest of electric wires touching the back of my neck, sending warm sensations through me. Then, as the lights flare, a scar against the blue-
40 black sky, I see Shoeless Joe Jackson standing out in left field. His feet spread wide, body bent forward from the waist, hands on hips, he waits. I hear the sharp crack of the bat, and Shoeless Joe drifts effortlessly a few steps to his left, raises his right hand to
45 signal for the ball, camps under it for a second or two, catches it, at the same time transferring it to his throwing hand, and fires it into the infield.

I make my way to left field, walking in the darkness far outside the third-base line, behind where the
50 third-base stands would be. I climb up on the wobbly bleacher behind the fence. I can look right down on Shoeless Joe. He fields a single on one hop and pegs the ball to third.

I lean back and watch the game. From where I sit
55 the scene is as complete as in any of the major-league baseball parks I have ever visited: the two teams, the stands, the fans, the lights, the vendors, the scoreboard.

Home Game

When he was a kid, he'd be up at five
Take shots till eight, make the thing drive
Out after school, back on the ice
That was his life,
He was gonna play in the Big League
The Big League . . .

Tom Cochrane, "Big League"

Hockey will never hold the monopoly of time and attention it once held in Saskatchewan and Canada. Yet people still have a need to come together – in Radisson and Churchbridge, in Saskatoon, Toronto,
5 and Montreal – to feel close, to share something in common. Look around at the crowd this snowbound night in Saskatoon. Amidst a variety of people of different ages and generations, there are a father and his daughter; a young girl, probably a university
10 student, and her boyfriend; a grandmother and granddaughter and the grandmother's friend – young and old, male and female, city people and country people, businessmen, mine workers, and farmers. In no other place in Saskatoon do so many people of so
15 many different backgrounds gather together so often. And if Saskatoon can never be Swift Current or Prince Albert, SaskPlace and the Blades [the

Saskatoon hockey team] can make it feel that way sometimes. In a few months from now at the
20 Memorial Cup, these people will be back — louder, more passionate, and in even greater numbers.

To this community, hockey is part of a shared imagination. Even among those who don't watch it or play it or care about it in any way, it is *there*. Water and
25 pavement and airwaves and steel are instruments of that community, and so is the hockey arena. But move inside the arena on a Friday night or Saturday morning, or practically any time between November and March almost any place in the country. Come to
30 SaskPlace for the Memorial Cup in May, for a hockey game, and there you find a community of the spirit, a feeling that binds.

Extract 3

This passage is from *Tennis Love*, a book written by former tennis pro Billie Jean King and Greg Hoffman.

Tennis Love

Neither of my parents played tennis. As a matter of fact, I wasn't able to talk my dad into picking up a racket until 1968, nearly fifteen years after I started playing. When the tennis establishment officially
5 recognized the pro element, he finally consented to give it a try. Until then, he considered tennis to be a pastime for the country-club set, a view shared by many people.

That image, of course, has changed considerably
10 in recent years. The great majority of youngsters flocking to tennis courts today are doing so because of a prior exposure to the game, most likely either by television or by their parents.

As an example of the latter, I know one couple
15 who introduced their son to tennis well before he reached his first birthday. Whenever they went out to play, the couple would hang the baby's portable car seat, with the infant firmly strapped therein, on the chain link fence which enclosed the court.
20 Apparently believing that it was totally natural to be hung up in that manner, the child offered no protest. In fact, he rather enjoyed it.

Before long, however, the child outgrew his unique ringside seat. No problem. He became the family's
25 official ball boy, a position he initially filled with enthusiasm if not grace. He was thrilled by his contribution to the proceeding, and as time went on, he became highly competent in the performance of his duties. Then, just about the time he began to tire of
30 chasing the balls, his parents presented him with a racket. They lost a ball boy, but gained a tennis player.

There are few sports more ideally suited to children than good ol' tennis. It is neither time-consuming nor prohibitively expensive. Also, tennis is a non-

Speaking

Pronunciation Practice

1. Sportscasters use intonation and pitch to demonstrate the excitement of the moment during their play-by-plays. Intonation is the pattern of sound changes produced by the rise and fall of our voices. The emotion of the speaker can be shown by changing the pitch (the degree of highness or lowness of a sound) within different intonation patterns. Excitement in English is shown by a rising intonation pattern. In addition, the content word that is the object of the excitement receives extra sentence stress.

Listen to the following sentences. Underline the stressed words and draw arrows to show the intonation patterns.

EXAMPLE: Strike three. You're out.

a) He shoots. He scores!

b) Going, going, gone – it's a home run.

c) The horses are neck and neck. Silver Streak has just taken the lead by a nose.

d) Shots up. What a rejection by Jones!

e) We have just witnessed the fastest 100 metres ever.

f) Schneider lines it up and lasers it at the goalie.

g) Goal – a great finish on that shot.

h) Another ace! Sampress has his big gun going today.

i) A great dig, but an even bigger spike!

j) Smith punches it into the end zone. Touchdown!

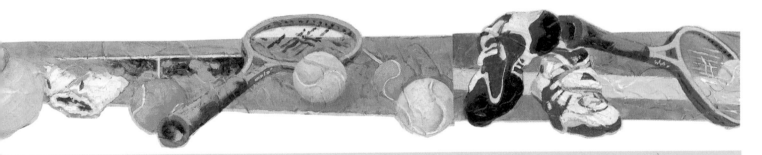

35 violent, non-contact sport, which is an important consideration for parents who are rightfully concerned with the physical well-being of the young athletes in the family. Since it is a technique sport, tennis offers the child not blessed with an overabun-
40 dance of natural athletic ability the opportunity to excel in an athletic endeavour.

One more factor that makes tennis especially well suited for children regardless of sex is that it is a predominantly individual sport. Team sports do provide
45 plenty of opportunity for a child to learn leadership and cooperation with others, but their basic structure can also lead a child to develop a tendency to pass the buck, to blame others for a poor showing instead of saying, "Hey, maybe I could do better."

2. Listen to the tape again and repeat each sentence. With a partner, practise reading the sentences with the stress and intonation patterns you have identified.

3. Try to identify the sports represented in each sentence.

Vocabulary 1

1. Sports are an important part of our culture. As a result, we have many expressions and idioms which are based on sports references. Fill in the blanks below with the unscrambled words and complete the crossword puzzle.

Across

1. I wasn't sure if I could go the _____ *(edcaitsn)* and finish my degree part-time after I started my family, but I managed to finally graduate.

2. The union is notorious for *playing* _____ *(dlhralba)* when it comes to wage negotiations; consequently, it usually gets a good deal for its members because it doesn't back down easily.

3. Since my grandmother fell and broke her hip last winter, her general health has been going steadily *down*_____ *(lilh)*.

4. Because of government financial cutbacks, post-secondary institutions have had to *(twerlse)* _____ *with the hard facts* and cut both programs and staff.

5. The candidates for the leader's position are *neck and* _____ *(knec)*. At this point nobody can really say who the winner will be.

Down

1. I know you can't give me an exact quote, but can you at least give me a *ballpark* _____ *(egfuir)* as to how much you think it will cost?

2. Even though it is a big job, Katalina has agreed *to* _____ *(eltkca)* the labelling and organization of all the photos I've taken over the last ten years because she loves a challenge.

3. If you have a minute, I'd like to _____ *(bcunoe) a few ideas* off you. I really value your opinion.

4. We've overcome all the major obstacles that we faced. From here on it's *clear* _____ *(iilsgna)*.

5. Mohamed *beat me to the* _____ *(hpucn)* and asked Yasmine to the dance before I could.

2. Working in teams of four or five, discuss the idioms in the crossword puzzle. Which sports do you think they originated from?

3. For five minutes, brainstorm as many sports idioms as possible. Compare your results with those of other teams and give your team a point for each idiom your team found that no other team has.

Listening 1

T8.b

You will hear a typical North American parent being interviewed about his family's participation in sports.

Before You Listen

Complete the following chart by surveying your classmates for the appropriate information.

Focused Listening

Now listen for the answers to these questions.

1. What are two commitments that parents must make to have their children involved in hockey?

2. What are three benefits of participating in hockey as a youth?

3. What two benefits do parents receive from having their children on a sports team?

One Step Beyond

Read the two opposing opinions below about the role of violence in sports.

Opinion #1

I'm against any violence in sports. All sports that encourage or tolerate violence should be banned. The problem begins with children playing hockey, soccer, even baseball. The organizers of these sports for children say the sports are not competitive. One coach told me that sports encourage children to challenge their own limits. It's not true. The games are built around competitions and no one wants to be a loser. Many parents encourage kids to do whatever it takes to win. The worst thing is that kids grow up believing that violence is "cool" and a sign of being good in sports. How can kids ever learn to handle conflict constructively if the message they get from the sports world is that violence is okay? Sports that tolerate violence contradict the purpose of sporting events, which is to demonstrate "good sportsmanship." Somehow we've forgotten what that means.

Individual or Team Sport	Equipment Required	Approximate Cost of Equipment	Support Needed from Parents
Soccer			
Baseball			
Tennis			
Hockey			
Swimming			

Opinion #2

I'm not sure that violence in sports is such a bad thing. First of all, let's face it, we all have to deal with a lot of stress in our lives – at school, at home, at work. Even kids have a lot of stress these days. Playing a sport in which it's okay to let out your frustrations in a punch or two is a great way to release some of that negative energy. We keep wanting to deny that we feel anger. We do feel anger and isn't it better to let that anger out on the sports field rather than on the street or at home? Violence in sports is a controlled violence. All sports set some limits to violence. Sure, some sports tolerate more than others. But even the most violent sports have referees that will stop the fighting if it gets out of hand. I think it's much better to let out that excess energy and frustration on the sports field in a controlled environment than let it build up inside you and then lash out uncontrollably.

1. In point form, jot down other pros and cons of violence in sports not expressed in the opinions.

2. Divide into two teams and debate the topic.

riting

Write a paragraph supporting your opinion about violence in sports.

Grammar Focus 1

BASE + ING VERBALS

In addition to the main verb of the sentence, verbs can be used in other positions in the sentence when they don't have a tense. When a verb is used without a tense, it is called a *verbal*. A verbal can be used alone, or more commonly, as part of a phrase.

The *base + ing* verbal is one common form of non-tense specific verbs in English. *Base + ing* verbals or verbal phrases suggest that an activity is in progress, rather than expected. In this form verbals are active in meaning, suggesting that someone or something is responsible for the action. *Base + ing* verbals can be used in two ways:

1. to name an action

   When the *base + ing* verbal names an action, it is used as a noun or noun phrase (gerund).

2. to describe someone or something

   In this case, the verbal describes the noun.

1. *Base + ing* **Verbals Naming an Action**

Verbals used as a noun or noun phrase can be placed in three sentence positions:

a) in the subject position

EXAMPLE: (Playing) pick-up is a popular pastime in many small communities.

In this example, the verbal phrase *playing pick-up* acts as the subject of the sentence.

b) in the object or complement position after certain verbs (For a list of verbs that take a gerund as object, see the Appendix on page 159.)

EXAMPLE: During my youth, I enjoyed (taking) swimming lessons.

c) after a preposition

EXAMPLE: You score points in this game by (throwing) the ball through the hoop.

In this case, the verbal phrase *throwing the ball through the hoop* follows the preposition *by*.

2. *Base + ing* **Verbals Describing a Noun**

Verbals used to describe a noun can be placed in four positions in the sentence:

a) as an insert, usually at the end of the sentence and separated by a comma (the verbal can also be used at the beginning of the sentence, but this is less common)

EXAMPLE: Many youngsters play hockey, (hoping) to join the big leagues some day.

In this example, the *base + ing* verbal phrase describes the noun *youngsters*.

b) as a post-modifier in a noun phrase. In this case, the verbal describes an action of the noun it follows. We understand that the noun itself is responsible for the action described.

EXAMPLE: On sunny days, there are many *couples* (playing) tennis at the park.

c) as an adjective in the complement position after *be* or other linking verbs

EXAMPLE: Hitting the final winning run of the game *was* (exhilarating.)

d) as a pre-modifier in a noun phrase
   In this position, the verbal relates to the noun that follows in two distinct ways depending on what the noun and the verbal mean:

   i) the verbal describes what the noun does and the noun is responsible for the action

   EXAMPLE: Soccer is an (exciting) *game*.

   In this sentence, the game itself is exciting.

   ii) the verbal describes the noun, but the noun is not responsible for the action

   EXAMPLE: Thomas spends all his free time in the (batting) *cage*.

   In this sentence, the cage itself is not batting (it doesn't do the batting, rather it is *for* batting). The verbal is used to classify the noun as a type of cage.

Exercise A

1. Identify the *base + ing* verbals in the following passage. Where applicable, indicate the nouns the verbals are describing.

Playing sports is an important part of growing up. On the weekends, playing fields throughout the community are full of people of all ages participating in interesting sports. Hoping to be star athletes, many youths dedicate themselves to long hours of practice. However, few can really expect to reach international stardom.

Being at the top of a sport requires a lot of hard work, talent, and dedication. When training, athletes build their endurance by practising their sports for long, exhausting hours. They do not mind dedicating their lives to their professions because they enjoy pushing their performances to the peak of their abilities. Before major competitions, athletes avoid taking part in any activities that might distract them, hoping not to risk losing their competitive edge. At important competitions, you can often see athletes giving the best performances of their careers because they are totally "psyched" for the competition. As a result, they tend to be very single-minded and refuse to let anything stand in the way of achieving their goals. They have chosen to dedicate themselves wholeheartedly to their sports, which for them are thrilling.

2. In the passage, find examples of each type of *base + ing* verbal outlined in the grammar explanation.

Tip

Look back at each sentence that contains the *base + ing* verbals. Notice that although verbals are not time specific, generally they refer to an action that has already happened, is in progress, or is about to occur.

Exercise B

Build sentences from the following phrases using an appropriate verbal.

EXAMPLE: *practise*: six hours a day / common / professional figure skaters.

Practising six hours a day is common amongst professional figure skaters.

Grammar Focus 1

1. *watch:* Sports fans / enjoy / fast-paced basketball game.
2. *score:* Kyle / won / most valuable player award / most goals in the tournament.
3. *try :* Elvis / practise / quadruple every day / perfect the landing.
4. *climb:* many children / enjoy / playground equipment / park.
5. *thrill:* was / participate / Olympic team.
6. *run:* athletes / have / custom-made / shoes.

Grammar In Use

When I was younger, I used to go to the park with my dad and kick around the soccer ball. He was a really good soccer player and played professionally when he was in his twenties. He taught me to head the ball and carry the ball down the field with good footwork. We also enjoyed challenging each other to basketball games. He usually outplayed me in soccer, we were pretty even in basketball, but I liked playing tennis with him because I usually won. I liked summer sports better than winter sports. I guess I really never liked the cold all that much and I thought hockey was too violent. Have you seen how many hockey players are missing their front teeth? It's right up there with boxing on my list of sports I will never participate in.

I think participation in sports is a fun way to keep physically fit. My wife and I try to get in at least a few sets of tennis a week. My daughter is just three now and I've already started training her to kick the soccer ball and catch a baseball. I plan on spending lots of time with her at the park, chasing her around the playground and teaching her some soccer and baseball basics. Maybe in a few years we'll be able to beat her grandfather in a soccer game.

Based on the passage above, answer the following questions. Note how often verbals are used in the answers.

1. What are some physical activities that the writer enjoyed as a child?
2. What activities does the writer enjoy now?
3. What does the writer consider dangerous? What does the writer think he risks if he takes part in these sports?
4. What does the writer consider important? What is he determined to do to keep fit during the next year?

Reading 2

You will read a passage about the history of the Olympic Games from a book entitled *The Name of the Game.*

Before You Read

1. Working in teams of four or five, check your Olympic sports knowledge. In the chart on the next page, match the athletes in Column A with their accomplishments in Column B. Then check your answers on page 158.

   Now discuss the following questions.

2. What do the Olympic rings symbolize?
3. Where did the modern Olympics originate?
4. What famous Olympic athletes have come from your native country?
5. Do the Olympics stand for the same principles today as they did in the past?
6. Should professional athletes be allowed to participate in the Olympics? Why or why not?

Scanning

Quickly scan the article for the following facts.

a) the name of the cook who won the first race in 776 BC _____

b) the prize that Coroebus won _____

c) the origin of the word *Olympics*

   _____

d) the name of the person responsible for the end of the ancient Olympics _____

e) the number of athletes who took part in the first modern Olympics _____

f) the year figure skating became part of the Olympics _____

Column A	Column B
1) Donovan Bailey	a) Norwegian who won two golds and two silvers in cross-country skiing in 1994
2) Sergei Bubka	b) Chinese woman who won the women's table tennis gold medal in 1988
3) Bjorn Dahlie	c) Ethiopian who won the 5000 and 10 000 metre races in 1980
4) Greg Louganis	d) American who won the 3 metre springboard and 10 metre highboard diving competitions at the 1984 Olympics
5) Jing Chen	e) East German speedskater who won two gold medals and two silver medals in 1984
6) Earvin "Magic" Johnson	f) Canadian who won the 100 metre dash at the 1996 Olympics in Atlanta
7) Miruts Gifter	g) British pair who were Olympic figure skating champions in 1984 and also four-time world champions
8) Jayne Torvill and Christopher Dean	h) star American player on the basketball "Dream Team" that won gold in 1992
9) Karen Enke	i) Ukrainian who won the pole vault and set a new Olympic record in 1988
10) Kristi Yamaguchi	j) American who won the women's figure skating gold in 1992 at Albertville

he Name of the Game

Pity the spectator who dropped his program at the first Olympic Game. As he stooped to pick it up, he probably missed the main event. It was a foot race lasting less than 30 seconds! And it was the *only*
5 athletic event of the day because that original race at Olympia, Greece, in 776 BC was part of a big religious ceremony held in honour of Zeus, the top-ranked Greek god.

The winner of the race, Coroebus, was a cook
10 from the nearby town of Elis, and thus became the very first Olympic champion. He and several other runners sprinted naked (a custom at the time) on a sandy track 630 feet [192 m] long. The distance was a Greek measure called a *stade*, from which we get
15 our modern word *stadium*.

Why was a foot race a religious ceremony? Next to their many gods and goddesses, the ancient

Greeks revered athletic skill above all things. They reasoned that the best way to honour the gods was to develop discipline in body and mind. Since a big festival and ceremony were held for Zeus every four years at Olympia, somebody got the idea of staging a race with the fastest sprinters from several towns and cities in the running.

As years passed, more athletic events were added. The original foot race in which Coroebus won himself a crown of laurel leaves became known as the Olympic Games, and cities all over Greece sent their best athletes there to "win their laurels" too. Eventually the athletic activities became more important than the ceremony for Zeus as thousands of spectators jammed into the stadium to cheer their favourites.

Don't get the idea that the Olympic Games were named for Olympia, the town where the games were first held, or even for Mount Olympus, the mythical home of the gods, which is several hundred miles away. The name comes from the Greek word *olympiad*, which stands for a period of time spanning four years. The festivals to Zeus and the athletic games that were to make them even more popular were held every four years at a site selected for Zeus's temple in a beautiful valley beside a winding river. Once the games were established, they were repeated every four years for the next 1200 years. At first, only a few nearby towns got in the act. But the popularity – and rivalry for Olympic laurels – soon spread across Greece, and from there to other lands and islands such as Rhodes, Crete, Sicily, Egypt, and Asia Minor. More athletic events were introduced into the Games as participation grew.

Everybody wanted to make a good showing at the temple of Zeus every four years and carry off the Olympic laurels. It was better to beat rival cities in races and boxing matches than to clobber them with swords and spears. Thus, there was a relatively peaceful period every time the Games were held. Fighting usually stopped as warriors went to show off their skills in more peaceful competitions. And in many instances, the wars didn't resume when the Games were over. Too bad this wasn't the case during World War I and World War II, when the Olympic Games were suspended instead of the battles.

Eventually the Games at Olympia did come to an end. The Romans conquered Greece in 146 BC and continued to hold athletic competitions there for a few more centuries, but the Games began to go downhill. One story tells us that the Roman emperor Nero himself entered some of the events, but intimidated his opponents to gain an advantage. In one instance, he entered a chariot race while drunk. No one would compete against him, and even though he fell out of his chariot and couldn't finish the race, he was declared the winner. Emperors can get away with that sort of thing it seems.

Finally, in 393 AD, Emperor Theodosius I, who had been converted to Christianity, blew the whistle on the Games because, he said, they were pagan activities and a "public nuisance." Even the "eternal flame" in the Temple of Zeus was put out, and the Olympic stadium and surrounding buildings were either torn down or left to destruction by floods and earthquakes. It took 15 centuries to get the Olympic Games going again.

April 6, 1896 is the date of the start of the modern Olympic Games. It happened in Athens, Greece, but the man most responsible for the revival of the games was a go-ahead French baron named Pierre de Coubertin. Though only five feet, three inches [160 cm] tall and not an athlete himself, Coubertin nevertheless managed almost single-handedly to promote the idea of an international amateur athletic competition patterned after the original Olympics.

Compared to today's Games, the first modern Olympics in 1896 wouldn't make much of a show. Only 311 athletes from 13 nations were entered. Compare that with more than 8000 athletes from about 40 countries who show up for the summer and winter Olympics these days. There were 40 events in the 1896 program.

Many thousands of Olympic medals have been won since that great day in Athens near the turn of this century. The variety and quality of Olympic competition have grown as more and more nations joined in. Records by the score have been broken and re-broken. The first winter sport, figure skating, was introduced in London in 1908, and the Olympic Winter Games were begun as a separate competition at Chamonix, France in 1914.

For Discussion

Working in teams of four or five, describe five significant changes that have taken place since the modern Olympics began.

Writing

Write a short comparison/contrast essay about some of the significant changes your team identified. You can choose one of two approaches. For example, you may compare point-by-point. If you are describing the original games and the modern games, you would refer to both when making each point. Or, you may write all about one aspect (original) and then all about the contrasting aspect (modern). Sometimes the comparisons/contrasts in this type of approach are not quite as clear to the reader.

Grammar Focus 2

BASE + ING VERBALS (GERUNDS) VS. INFINITIVES

1. Gerund or Infinitive?

To determine whether a *to + base* verbal (infinitive) or a *base + ing* verbal (gerund) is needed, consider the following.

1. Does the verbal complement follow any of the verbs listed in the Appendix (page 159) that usually take the *to + base* or the *base + ing* verbal?

2. Does the complement indicate an action that preceeded or is in progress at the same time as the main verb (*base + ing* verbal), or does it indicate an action that is possible or has a sense of future (*to + base* verbal)?

3. Does the verbal follow a preposition? Only *base + ing* verbals can follow a preposition.

4. Is the verbal in the subject position? The *to + base* verbal and *base + ing* verbal are both possible in the subject position, although *base + ing* is more common (with "it," however, use the infinitive).

Exercise A

Using your knowledge of how *base + ing* and infinitive verbals are used, complete the following sentences with the appropriate form of the verb in brackets.

1. _____ *(collect)* hockey cards is a popular hobby for young kids.

2. Kyle promised _____ *(get up)* without a fuss for hockey practice at 5 a.m.

3. The tennis pro intends _____ *(earn)* millions for endorsing Nike™ shoes.

4. My sister enjoys _____ *(play)* basketball with my friends.

5. Everyone expects Carlos _____ *(win)* the tournament.

6. Athletes cannot risk _____*(injure)* themselves before major meets.

7. It's important _____ *(practice)* consistently if you want to improve your game.

8. Have you finished _____ *(prepare)* the field for the game yet?

9. What about _____ *(bat)* left-handed?

10. Tennis is considered _____ *(be)* a game of skill.

2. Differences in Meaning

Certain verbs can be followed by either the *base + ing* verbal or the infinitive form, however, there can be a difference in meaning. *Base + ing* verbal complements are often used to show that the action has taken place *before* the action of the main verb, or that the action is in progress *at the same time* as the main verb.

EXAMPLE: Juan stopped going to English class when he got a part-time job.

Juan was going to English class (action 1) and then he stopped (action 2).

Infinitive verbal complements are often used to show that the action is in the future or not real. The verbal is used to show that the action has taken place *after* the action of the main verb.

EXAMPLE: Juan stopped to pick up milk on the way home.

Juan stopped (action 1) and then he picked up milk (action 2).

Grammar Focus 2

The following main verbs can take either the gerund or infinitive form as a complement, however, the meaning is different: *remember, forget, regret, stop.*

Exercise B

Working in teams of two or three, discuss how the following pairs of sentences differ in meaning. Note which event is first and which is second.

1. a) Did you remember to order pizzas for the team party?

   b) Do you remember ordering pizzas for the team party?

2. a) I forgot to wash my soccer uniform.

   b) I forgot washing my soccer uniform.

3. a) Raphael stopped kicking the ball.

   b) Raphael stopped to kick the ball.

4. a) We regret to inform you that you did not make the team.

   b) We regret informing you that you did not make the team.

Grammar In Use

THREE STRIKES – YOU'RE OUT!

Divide into two teams. Each team member should attempt to build a grammatically correct sentence which contains a verbal using the words provided. If the sentence is correct, your team scores a run. No main verb can be used twice. If the sentence is incorrect or uses a main verb already used, your team gets a strike. The inning is finished when each member of the team has made a sentence or the team has received three strikes.

Team A			
Main Verbs		**Verbs**	
advise	continue	eat	hear
finish	miss	pay	win
begin	remember	clean	study
hope	permit	register	lose
risk	fail	see	stop

Team B			
Main Verbs		**Verbs**	
allow	neglect	purchase	present
refuse	detest	listen	drink
avoid	propose	give up	do
intend	used to	walk	say
love	enjoy	meet	sit

Vocabulary 2

1. Sports fanatics like to let the world know of their passion for sports or their special sports accomplishments. One way to do this is to have a special vanity licence plate on their car. Determine what the following sports vanity plates mean by sounding out the letters and looking for other clues.

EXAMPLE: KCHR = catcher

a) BYANZ
b) HOLN1
c) BULZI
d) 25BK
e) 4WRD
f) HVW8
g) RITGRD
h) GR8ST
i) PCHR
j) 10SPRO
k) GOLE

[Check your answers on page 158.]

2. Onomatopoeic words are words that sound like what they mean. Listen to the following words and number them in order as you hear them. Do you think the words sound like what they mean?

slices ( )   groaned ( )
dribbled ( )   smashed ( )
slap ( )   roar ( )
slammed ( )   booted ( )
pop ( )   tap ( )

3. Complete the following sentences using words from the list above.

a) Michael Jordan _____ the basketball down the court and then _____ it in the hoop.

b) Tiger Woods rarely _____ the ball — he usually gets so close to the hole that he only needs to _____ it in with a single stroke.

c) The fans _____ when the soccer player _____ the ball in his own net.

d) In his last at bat, Roger hit a _____ fly which the backcatcher easily caught. This time he _____ the ball way out into left field.

e) To the _____ of the crowd, John took a _____ shot from the corner and got the winning goal.

*L*istening 2

Before You Listen

Working in teams of four or five, discuss the following.

1. How do you think sports such as archery, wrestling, track and field, and weightlifting began?

2. What sports originated in the countries of your teammates?

Focused Listening

You will hear a number of short passages about the possible origins of various sports. As you listen, complete the following chart.

	Origin	**Date of Origin**	**Interesting Point**
Bowling			
Wrestling and Boxing			
Soccer			
Lacrosse			
Basketball			
Golf			

For Discussion

1. Sports today are played mainly for recreation. Why did we start playing sports and how has the role of sports in society changed?

2. What other games does your team know the origins of?

3. Should any sport be eligible for inclusion in the Olympics? Why or why not?

One Step Beyond

Working in teams of three or four, devise a new game that uses the following equipment.

- 4 large laundry detergent boxes
- 6 large juice tins
- a tennis ball
- 6 metresticks

Write the rules for the game and be prepared to teach the game to your classmates.

*U*nit Reflection

This unit is called "It's How You Play the Game." How appropriate is this title to both individual and team sports? Are there other aspects of our lives where this expression would apply?

Unit 9

Food For Thought

DISCUSSION

Choose a photo and caption below that interests you and discuss it with a partner.

Who or what is responsible for world hunger?

What role does food play in our lives?

What is proper nutrition?

London, Paris, New York or Somalia?

Because of the tremendous pressure to be thin, many female models starve themselves. To the point where they end up anorexic, bulimic or, in very extreme cases, dead. Next time you go on a diet, ask yourself, who are you modelling yourself after? The National Eating Disorder Information Centre. It's not our bodies that need changing. It's our attitudes. College Wing 1-211, 200 Elizabeth St. Toronto Ontario M5G 2C4.

What cultural factors encourage eating disorders?

How do supermarkets compare in various countries?

Before You Read

You will read an excerpt from a book chapter entitled "The Big Business of Food." Before you read, test your food trivia knowledge by trying the following quiz.

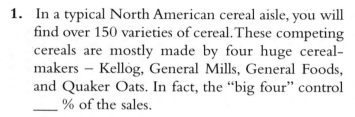

A Shopper's Quiz

1. In a typical North American cereal aisle, you will find over 150 varieties of cereal. These competing cereals are mostly made by four huge cereal-makers – Kellog, General Mills, General Foods, and Quaker Oats. In fact, the "big four" control ____ % of the sales.

    a) 50

    b) 90

    c) 75

2. For every dollar the food shopper spends, the farmer gets an average of about

    a) 35 cents.

    b) 55 cents.

    c) 75 cents.

3. Processed food is more profitable than fresh food because

    a) it is cheaper to produce.

    b) it can be sold in bulk.

    c) it has a longer shelf life.

4. Impulse buying (purchasing items you did not plan to buy when you entered the store) accounts for _____ % of total supermarket sales.

    a) 70

    b) 50

    c) 35

5. The most advantageous place for a product to be placed is

    a) under bright lights.

    b) at eye level.

    c) close to the cash register.

6. Sixty-five percent of all baby food sold in North America is

    a) Heinz.

    b) Farley's.

    c) Gerber.

7. Stores can afford "loss leaders" (special sale items advertised below cost) because

    a) the stores make money if they sell a lot.

    b) almost no one leaves the store without making other purchases.

    c) the manufacturer gives them money.

8. UPC stands for

    a) universal product code.

    b) under-preserved cans.

    c) unique purchase carton.

Check your answers on page 158. Then discuss the answers with a partner. Was there anything you found surprising?

The Big Business of Food

Ten thousand different items line the shelves, fill the bins, and are displayed in the freezer, meat, and dairy cases of our favourite supermarkets. So it's rather hard to believe that we are in any way limited as to
5 what we can buy once we've walked through the magic-eye doors into the temperature-controlled, fluorescent-lit, piped-music atmosphere of one of the massive stores.

Just take a stroll down the cereal aisle. You'll find as
10 many as 150 different kinds of ready-to-eat cereal and dozens of kinds of cooking cereals. Soda and soft drinks, canned soups and vegetables, macaroni products, cake mixes, salad dressings, frozen dinners, baby food, catfood, and dogfood also appear in
15 great variety, as do food items in scores of other categories. If that isn't choice, what is?

On the other hand, have you ever wondered why it's so difficult to find fresh peas in the pod or fresh rhubarb in season in the produce department, fresh-
20 killed rather than frozen turkeys even at Thanksgiving time, or more than two or three varieties of so-called fresh fish (more often prefrozen and thawed rather than truly fresh)? Why are there 30 or more different brands of beer in the store but only a
25 couple of different kinds of apples – usually Delicious and McIntosh – in a land that as recently as the 1960s grew and marketed more than 25 commercial apple varieties, each a unique eating experience?

The answer lies in the powerful control of our food
30 supply by giant companies that decide what will be marketed and what you and I will eat solely on the basis of profitability – theirs. With the packaging revolution, the advances in food technology, and the resulting onslaught of convenience and junk foods,
35 there is much more money to be made from the sale of highly processed, mass-produced, standardized food than from fresh foods. The latter, unless they are sold quickly, are highly perishable, while frozen and other processed foods have a long storage and shelf
40 life.

Consumers in North American supermarkets have a wide choice of products – or do they?

Even if a small farm half a [kilometre] down the road from a giant supermarket tried to sell its fresh produce, newly laid eggs, or freshly killed chickens to the store's manager, chances are the farmer would be
45 turned down flat, for the big chain stores and the major food wholesalers have special trade arrangements, and interlopers are not welcome. If independent suppliers offer better quality and more variety in fruits, vegetables, poultry, eggs, dairy products, and
50 other items, they are doubly unwelcome.

Once inside the supermarket, we are in the tightly governed realm of the big food corporations. At first glance it may appear that those heavily stocked shelves of breakfast foods and other products are a
55 battleground of the brands. But a closer look will usually reveal that numerous "competing" products are made by the very same company, and that a few

Farmers grow what their buyers, the large food companies, demand. This has led to a lack of diversification of crops.

giant corporations control the entire market.

Corporate control of the food we eat not only robs the consumer of a real variety of choices, reduces quality, and fixes prices through the elimination of meaningful competition, but it also robs the farmer of a competitive market for his products and dictates what the farmer must grow. Few farmers have the opportunity to sell directly to the public, and none can afford to grow what the food packers and processors refuse to buy.

So farmers obediently grow firm, bruise-resistant tomatoes, rot-resistant lettuce, and the kinds of peas, green beans, corn, and other vegetables that are best for canning or freezing, even though they may not be the most tender or flavourful varieties. In spite of hard work, efficient management, and modern mechanized equipment, today's independent farmer is being squeezed out by rising production costs, limited markets, the built-in risk of poor weather, losses due to lack of diversification of crops, and a steadily declining share of the consumer dollar.

When it comes to processed foods, the farmer's share is even smaller. The family of a dairy farmer pays at least five times more for an ice cream cone than it received for the milk that went into it; a wheat farmer pays at least eight times more for a loaf of bread than the amount of money that was received for the wheat.

So every time a consumer buys a package of processed food, most of what he or she spends tumbles into the widening gap between the farmer and the consumer. It is the food-processing industry that reaps the principal benefit. And because of high profitability, food processors are encouraged to pursue an even vaster market by expanding their range of products.

New products are the lifeblood of the food industry. Not content with offering simply processed foods like canned fruit cocktail and frozen meat patties, the food industry has also given us those hundreds of complex convenience foods with which we are all familiar – dehydrated mixes, synthetic juices, non-dairy creamers, and "instant" breakfasts that taste like candy bars.

So the consumer needs to tread with care along the well-stocked aisles of today's supermarkets. Studies also show that impulse buying – the purchase of items you did not plan on getting when you entered the store – accounts for up to 70 percent of supermarket sales.

Supermarket planners have mapped out the traffic patterns shoppers will follow as they walk around the store. Shelf displays have been set up accordingly, with the big food companies usually acquiring the best locations, designed to attract the attention at eye level in the best-lighted and most-frequented aisles. Small impulse items like candy and gum are, of course, displayed near the checkout lines to catch the eye of impatient adults and clamouring children.

No matter how educated one might be, it remains difficult for the average consumer to avoid all those enticements and traps that big business has spent a fortune on. Whether we like it or not, what we put in our mouths everyday has been strongly influenced by the politics of big food industries.

Scanning for Information

List the facts supporting the idea that consumer buying habits are manipulated by the food industry.

Summarizing

The ability to summarize an article or text is an important skill. When summarizing, the goal is to explain briefly the main points of the reading in your own words. Therefore, the summary should be about one-quarter the length of the original text at most.

Below are a number of sentences that can be used to summarize the main ideas of the article you have just read. They are not in the order that the ideas appear in the article, but a summary does not have to reflect the exact order of ideas – just the ideas in general. Also, some sentences below do not relate to content in the article.

Using only appropriate sentences from those provided below, write a brief summary of the article. You may need to add sentence connectors or short transition sentences to make your summary coherent.

a) A very small portion of the price we pay for a product in the supermarket goes to the farmer who produced the food. Most goes to the intermediaries such as processors, packagers, truckers, etc.

b) Food corporations are researching high protein food substitutes called analogs that will produce high profits for them.

c) Big business controls every aspect of our shopping experience from the availability of products to their placement on the shelf.

d) Farmers have little direct access to supermarkets, so they are forced to grow what large corporations will buy.

e) The consumer pays less for many products because the big corporations can produce processed foods cheaper than small companies.

f) The development of new, highly processed, profitable products is mostly controlled by a few large corporations.

g) Supermarkets carry a high percentage of processed or frozen foods because they are less perishable than fresh foods and therefore more profitable.

h) Marketers place most popular foods at eye level in highly frequented aisles.

V ocabulary 1

1. Find words in the reading "The Big Business of Food" to complete the definitions below.

a) An _____ is someone who becomes involved in a situation without being asked or wanted.

b) To _____ carefully is to proceed or behave cautiously.

c) The _____ is the general mood created in a place.

d) Something that is _____ decays or rots quickly.

e) An _____ is a sudden strong desire to act, usually without thinking about the results.

f) A _____ experience is unusual or special in some way.

g) An _____ is a powerful, continuous presentation of something (almost an assault).

h) An _____ is something pleasant or attractive used to attract or tempt a person.

i) To _____ is to command or control someone or something.

j) _____ is the variation of things.

2. Look at the words as they appear in the context of the reading. Identify whether they are used as nouns, verbs, or adjectives and write them in the appropriate columns below.

Nouns	Verbs	Adjectives

3. For the ten words that you have studied in this exercise, write the noun, verb, adjective, and adverb forms where appropriate and use each in a sentence.

riting

Marketing plays a tremendous role in influencing how we shop and what we eat. Health care professionals have identified the need to reduce the level of fat in children's diets; however, over the past five years, advertising of "junky" foods during children's TV programs has increased from 16% to 41% of all food advertising. Marketing is part of doing business, but what responsibility do companies have for the health of our children? Write an editorial for your local newspaper outlining who should be responsible for children's health and nutrition and how businesses can encourage better nutrition amongst children.

S peaking

With a partner, complete the following opinion survey by responding with True (T) or False (F) to the following statements.

1. ☐ Women worry about their weight more than men do.

2. ☐ Men have a higher metabolism rate, so they don't have the same weight problems women have.

3. ☐ Women are as self-conscious as men about their manner of eating.

4. ☐ Men's and women's weights can affect their likelihood to be promoted at work.

5. ☐ Women are more likely to eat in secrecy than men.

6. ☐ Men burn off calories faster than women.

7. ☐ For biological reasons, women crave more fatty foods than men.

8. ☐ Men don't feel as guilty about overeating as women.

9. ☐ Men eat less junk food than women.

10. ☐ Women and men are equally likely to use food to reduce stress.

11. ☐ Men try to hide their poor eating habits from others.

12. ☐ Men and women have the same manner of eating in public restaurants.

13. ☐ Men don't like overweight women.

14. ☐ Men care as much about their appearance as women do.

15. ☐ Women don't like overweight men.

Compile the results from everyone in your class. Find the total number of people who answered true and false to each question and the total number of males and females who answered true and false to each question. Then discuss the following.

1. Did females respond differently to the survey than males? What are the most significant differences?

2. How is the psychology of eating different for men and women?

Illustrate the results of your class research in a chart or graph.

L istening 1

T9.a

You will hear a short lecture about some of the physical problems that can result from an abuse of food.

Before You Listen

In teams, discuss the following.

1. What role does food play in your life? Do you ever eat for comfort when you are sad or depressed? Do you ever eat out of boredom?

2. Famous individuals such as singer Karen Carpenter and Diana, Princess of Wales, suffered from eating disorders. Describe two eating disorders you are aware of. Do you know of any other famous people who have suffered from the disorders?

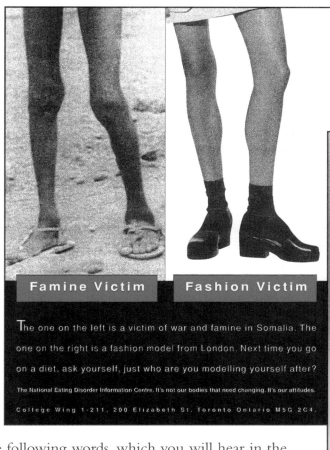

Famine Victim   **Fashion Victim**

The one on the left is a victim of war and famine in Somalia. The one on the right is a fashion model from London. Next time you go on a diet, ask yourself, just who are you modelling yourself after?

The National Eating Disorder Information Centre. It's not our bodies that need changing. It's our attitudes.

College Wing 1-211, 200 Elizabeth St. Toronto Ontario M5G 2C4.

3. The following words, which you will hear in the lecture, are often used in association with food. Discuss their meaning. If you are not familiar with any of the words, look them up in a dictionary.

sustenance	satiate	cope	purge
metabolic rate	binge		compulsive
addiction	gorge		obese

The model Twiggy set the standard for the thin female figure in the 1960s.

Focused Listening

As you listen, write point-form notes in response to the following questions.

1. What are three roles that food can play in people's lives?

2. Why are diets an unsuccessful way to lose weight?

3. What are two similarities between compulsive eating and alcoholism?

4. Describe three feelings that compulsive eaters have about food.

5. List at least four traits of the compulsive eater.

6. In the past, what were two things that women did to their bodies in order to be socially acceptable?

For Discussion

1. How can we encourage people to accept their body type and not try to emulate some elusive waif-like model?

2. What programs are you aware of to help with eating disorders?

3. What would you do if you discovered that your best friend had an eating disorder?

Grammar Focus

BASE + D/T/N VERBALS

In previous units, you have studied two different forms of verbals. In this unit, we look at one final form – the *base + d/t/n* or past participle form. Unlike *to + base* and *base + ing* verbals, these *base + d/t/n* verbals are passive in meaning. They suggest that people or things experience or are affected by an action. That is, the people or things they describe are themselves not *responsible* for the action.

EXAMPLE: I found a *half-eaten* bag of cookies stuffed behind some boxes of cereal.

Exercise A

Refer back to the reading "The Big Business of Food." Identify all of the *base + d/t/n* verbals in the first two paragraphs. You should find six verbals.

1. Sentence Positions of *Base + d/t/n* Verbals

Base + d/t/n verbals are commonly placed in the following positions in the sentence:

a) as a pre-modifier in a noun phrase
In this case, the verbal describes the "experience" of the noun, but the noun isn't responsible for the action.

EXAMPLE: Consumers purchase a lot of (processed) food.

Who did the processing? The food didn't process itself; someone else processed it.

b) as a post-modifier in a noun phrase
In this case, the verbal is used as part of a reduced relative clause.

EXAMPLE: *The diet product (introduced) to the market in January is selling well.*

Exercise B

Fill in the blanks with an appropriate verbal formed from the following verbs.

reduce	can	process	plan	control	burn

EXAMPLE: *freeze*
Many North Americans purchase *frozen* turkeys to cook for Thanksgiving dinner.

1. There must be at least 50 varieties of _____ soup available.

2. We eat a lot more _____ food than our parents did at our age.

3. Tightly _____ markets discourage farmers from growing some crops.

4. Fat- _____ products have become very popular.

5. The bakery cannot sell _____ baked goods.

6. Carefully _____ shopping routes entice consumers to buy more than they originally planned.

Tip

Here are some spelling tips when forming *base + d/t/n* verbals.

1. If a single syllable word ends with a single vowel + consonant, double the consonant and add *ed*. (e.g., can = canned)

   This rule also applies to two syllable words when the stress is on the second syllable.

   Do not double a final consonant *x* or *y*.

2. If a word ends with a consonant + *y*, change the *y* to *i* and add *ed*. (e.g., carry = carried)

3. For regular verbs with other patterns than those mentioned above, use *base + ed*.

Exercise C

Create sentences from the following words placing the verbal in an appropriate place.

EXAMPLE: *wrap*: fruit / decorative cellophane / most expensive
The fruit wrapped in decorative cellophane is the most expensive.

1. *stack:* cereal / floor/ on sale

2. *locate:* superstores / across North America / popular / shop

3. *sell:* corn / dozen / costs $4

4. *bottle:* water / French Alps / popular beverage

5. *market:* diet pills / primarily for women / multi-million dollar industry

2. Additional Sentence Positions

Base + d/t/n verbals are also found in the following sentence positions:

a) as adjectives in the complement

EXAMPLE: Teenage girls are (worried) about having the ideal body.

In English, feeling something is thought of as being passive; we "experience" the feeling rather than "do" it.

Some common feelings include:

annoyed	interested
amazed	irritated
angered	intrigued
bored	relaxed
concerned	restricted
constrained	shocked
excited	surprised
exhilarated	terrified
frightened	worried
frustrated	

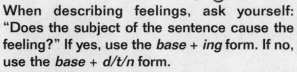

Tip

When describing feelings, ask yourself: "Does the subject of the sentence cause the feeling?" If yes, use the *base + ing* form. If no, use the *base + d/t/n* form.

EXAMPLE: "A *terrified* dog" means the dog is afraid.
"A *terrifying* dog" means the dog terrifies others.

b) as a descriptor of the subject (signals reason for the result expressed in the main clause)

EXAMPLE: (Influenced) by television advertisements, _young men_ eat chocolate bars thinking the bars will give them an energy boost.

As a result of being influenced by the media, the young men eat chocolate bars.

Exercise D

Fill in the blanks with the appropriate form of the word in brackets.

1. (*shock*) A _____ Maria couldn't believe what she had seen.

2. (*frustrate*) It is _____ for Juan that he cannot lose any weight.

3. (*bore*) It's a _____ experience to eat the same thing for breakfast every day.

4. (*surprise*) I was _____ to learn that so many people do not like their bodies.

5. (*interest*) An _____ Ali listened intently to the advertisement.

Exercise E

Combine the following sentences to form a new sentence containing a verbal.

1. Henry was enticed by the smell of fresh baking. He bought two dozen cookies.

2. Stores are designed by marketing experts. The stores are well-planned.

3. Felicity worries about her appearance. She goes on many crash diets.

4. Children are enticed by the shelves of candy. They beg their parents for treats.

5. Diet pills are often taken incorrectly. Diet pills can lead to serious health problems.

Exercise F

Identify the verbals in the following sentences and determine which pattern they fit.

1. Proven through many studies, the similarities between eating disorders and alcoholism are indisputable.

2. Coffee, grown on plantations in Colombia, is a favourite North American after-dinner beverage.

3. Convinced that thinness equals acceptance, countless women diet to achieve their elusive ideal weight.

4. Many women are frustrated by their inability to lose weight and keep it off.

5. Lisette was interested in the latest health food studies.

6. Fitness equipment designed to sculpt the perfect body is expensive.

7. The burnt brownie was still alluring for Geneva, who craved something sweet to eat.

8. Though loved by millions, Karen Carpenter starved herself to death.

9. A bored Nigel often eats junk food for something to do.

10. Richard Simmons, known as an exercise guru, was once extremely overweight and out of shape.

Grammar In Use

Gina has suffered from low self-esteem all her life. It started when she was in grade seven and some of her classmates began to tease her because she was a little overweight. Even though she was a pretty, fun-loving, intelligent girl, all she could focus on was her weight. She began to withdraw and kept to herself. Her personality changed dramatically and she no longer participated in extracurricular school activities. She started making herself throw up after every meal. Her parents worried about her. They took her to a counsellor. The counsellor helped Gina understand that everyone has different body types and that Gina's was fine the way it was. The counsellor explained that young girls were under tremendous pressure from the media to emulate an impossible perfect figure. Gina learned to accept herself and value what a truly special person she was. Since Gina learned that valuable lesson in her early teens, she has volunteered countless hours helping other young girls realize that, no matter what shape or size they may be, they are special and fine just the way they are.

Write at least eight sentences using *base + d/t/n* verbals based on the information in the paragraph.

Reading 2

You will read an excerpt from a book entitled *World Hunger: A Reference Handbook* which describes some of the facts and issues associated with the global hunger crisis.

Before You Read

In teams, discuss the following questions.

1. Despite advances in technology and improved farming techniques, millions of people continue to go hungry every day. Is this a result of natural forces or human will? Discuss the following quote:

   The Earth has enough for everyone's need but not enough for everyone's greed.
   – Mahatma Gandhi

2. What can you as an individual do to help alleviate world hunger?

3. How effective are social organizations at dealing with hunger problems?

Farmers in Asia, Africa, and Latin America produce a large proportion of the world's grain, yet these continents are also home to many of the world's hungry. Why?

The World Hunger Crisis

Men and women on the farms of Asia, Africa, and Latin America produced more than half of all the grain harvested in the world (in the 1989/90 crop year): 95% of the rice, 42% of the wheat, and 34% of grains such as maize, sorghum, and millet, called "coarse grains" in the language of the international grain trade. At the same time, despite ample world food supplies, at least half a billion people in those regions, about 10% of the earth's population, lacked enough food to eat, while another half billion lived at constant risk of hunger. This problem still exists today. The food missing in the daily lives of these millions amounts to a very small part of the world's annual harvest.

The great majority of the hungry live in rural areas — from 60% of hungry Latin Americans to 80% or even 90% of the hungry people in countries of Africa and Asia. Most of the world's underfed teenagers and most of the underfed mothers and fathers of hungry children help to grow and harvest the world's food. Nevertheless, they go hungry day after day, year after year. The greater part of the circumstances of their hunger is beyond their control and will remain beyond their control until the underlying causes of those circumstances change. Meanwhile, their lives wither away under hunger's relentless attack with scant attention from news media, policy makers, or the world in general. The tragedy of chronic hunger unfolds too slowly for the television camera, and it lacks the drama of famine.

As this is being written, news headlines warn of impending starvation for up to 8 million people in southern Sudan unless food reaches them quickly. Hostages to a long civil war, their agriculture has been destroyed by warring factions that also block trade and emergency relief coming from other countries. Warfare, directly and indirectly, accounts for much of the suffering of hunger today, as it has throughout history.

Headlines do not speak, however, of the 40 000 young children who will die of hunger-related deaths today and tomorrow and every day this year. They are dying in the Sudan, yes, but also in India, Pakistan, Bangladesh, the Philippines, Mozambique, Zaire, Uganda, Haiti, Bolivia, Honduras, and many other

Millions of children die each year from preventable illnesses and malnutrition. What are the solutions to this problem?

countries across the globe. Every year some 14 million children under the age of five, according to UNICEF and the World Health Organization, die from a combination of malnutrition and common illnesses, most of which can be prevented by relatively simple, low-cost methods.

Famine from the effects of war or other causes remains part of the world hunger problem. The lives blighted and brought to early death by chronic hunger, however, number not 8 million — monstrous as that figure is — but hundreds of millions.

Meanwhile, agricultural surpluses from North America and Europe depress the prices farmers the world over receive for their crops. This, too, is the world food problem: the sad paradox of many farmers being driven into debt (and eventually out of farming) by incomes that fail to cover even their farming costs, while millions of people go hungry for lack of food these same farmers produce. The problem of debt afflicts farmers in developing countries no less than farmers in the United States.

Hunger in a world of agricultural surplus makes no sense. World production of staple food is adequate to cover every person's basic caloric needs. Clearly something is terribly awry in the way the world is feeding (or not feeding) itself. That much everyone agrees.

Conventional wisdom knows that specialists from any one field of expertise need to listen carefully to the expertise of specialists also from other fields. Nutritionists, economists, anthropologists, political scientists, sociologists, public health workers, heads of state, community organizers, farmers, and agricultural scientists – all need to learn from one another, for no one profession and no one perspective has all the tools or all the answers needed to deal with hunger. More than ever before, the effort to end hunger is a cooperative venture among many different professions and institutions. Conventional wisdom is coming to recognize what people working at the grassroots long have known: that it is crucial to find out what the hungry themselves know about the causes and cures for their situation.

Wherever hunger persists and whatever the circumstances, there can be no adequate substitute for the wisdom of direct experience. Without the view from below, no perspective on the hunger problem can be complete.

Even as specialists continue to seek better knowledge and more workable solutions in each specific situation of hunger, nearly everyone agrees that what is known could eliminate most hunger already if only national governments put that knowledge into practice. Political will to rank the end of hunger high among national priorities is the most essential and the most sorely missing ingredient for solution of the world hunger problem – a will expressed in national budgets, policy decisions, and action, not just in rhetoric. In this case the persistence of hunger in a country like the United States greatly resembles the persistence of hunger in a country like India, Ethiopia, or Brazil.

Behind hunger stands poverty, and behind poverty stands powerlessness to bring about change. Powerlessness, in turn, has many roots: the absence of resources or assets to invest in change; the absence of sufficient health, energy, and vitality to apply even the knowledge and resources already at hand or to seek what is missing; and the absence of organization among the powerless to obtain collectively what they cannot do individually.

Another obstacle is the way those with relatively greater power use that power to keep their privileged status. Sometimes this abuse of power takes the form of violence or threats of violence to prevent the poor from organizing effectively or from acquiring resources and knowledge. More often it happens subtly. Interference with efforts by the poor to improve their situation is more flagrant, more violent, and more commonly tolerated or encouraged by officials in some societies than in others. To one degree or another, however, the operation of this obstacle should be suspected in any society with significant gaps between rich and poor.

By changing the way we use and distribute access to the Earth's resources, an additional nine billion people can be accommodated in good health and reasonable comfort. Agriculture, for example, must generate the soil's fertility, protect limited water resources, and produce crops by ecologically benign and sustainable means. Diets will need to obtain most of their calories and protein from grain directly instead of by feeding the grain first to animals where grain is converted into nutrients much less efficiently. Technology must rely on renewable resources with better technology found for recycling old products into new. Finally, broad-based economic growth and distributive equity must become higher social priorities than they are now in most countries. Values receive greater support from public policy and economic and social institutions.

One fact is very clear. Success in eliminating hunger comes more readily when both the hungry and the well-fed demand, and public policy recognizes and supports, what is actually needed. Neither knowledge without political will nor political will without insight will get the job done.

---

(7) *ample:* more than enough
(24) *wither:* become weak
(31) *impending:* going to happen soon
(34) *factions:* groups with different ideas than the main group
(50) *famine:* lack of food for a great number of people causing illness and death
(52) *blighted:* severely damaged
(56) *depress:* reduce the value
(80) *venture:* plan of action
(86) *persists:* continues to exist
(120) *flagrant:* obvious bad action
(130) *benign:* harmless

Comprehension Check

1. Which continents are home to most of the world's hungry?

2. Why aren't the media interested in the chronic hunger of the underfed who toil to grow and harvest the world's food?

3. What factor has proven to be one of the leading contributors to famine throughout human history?

4. How many children die each year from preventable causes?

5. Why are farmers going broke when there is such a shortage of food?

6. What are some possible solutions to world hunger?

7. What are some obstacles to significantly decreasing world hunger?

One Step Beyond

1. "Sometimes the abuse of power takes the form of violence or threats of violence . . . More often it happens subtly." What does the writer mean by this statement? Give examples.

2. Why is organization among the powerless so important to solving world hunger?

Writing

1. Write a brief summary of the reading. Your summary should consist of no more than one sentence per paragraph, but preferably less.

2. Write a short essay describing the relationship between poverty and world hunger.

Speaking

1. The World Health Organization has called together a committee of international youths to study the problem of world hunger and to make recommendations for solutions.

   As a committee of six to eight members, analyze the problem by considering population, environmental policies and economics, big business, and nature. Recommend solutions to the World Health Organization.

2. Prepare the outline of a report on your committee's findings which includes:

   - title
   - summary
   - background
   - analysis
   - recommendations

Exchange your findings with the other committees.

Vocabulary 2

A *suffix* is a group of letters that comes at the end of a word and is joined to the root. Sometimes the suffix adds meaning to the word. Other times the suffix is used to change the part of speech. Some common suffixes that you may know already are *-ful, -ly, -s, -less, -ity, -er, -al,* and *-ist.*

Scan through the reading "The World Hunger Crisis" carefully to find at least two words with the following suffixes. Complete the chart below by identifying the root and the meaning of the suffix.

Suffix	Words	Root	Meaning of Suffix
-ly			
-ist			
-al			
-ion			
-er			
-less			
-ness			
-ity			

One Step Beyond

What other words do you know that end with these suffixes? Find one new word for each suffix and write a sentence showing the meaning of your word.

Listening 2

You will hear an interview between a daytime talk show host and Dr. Manders, a leading expert on world poverty.

Before You Listen

During an interview, the interviewer and interviewee have specific responsibilities to carry out if the interview is to be a success. The following is a list of some of those responsibilities. Working in pairs, determine which are the responsibilities of the interviewer, which are the responsibilities of the interviewee, and which are the responsibilities of both.

- puts the guest at ease
- expresses himself or herself clearly
- uses specific language
- keeps control of the interview
- supports ideas with examples, illustrations, and anecdotes
- changes the topic
- clarifies
- uses clear and concise phrases
- answers the questions
- summarizes
- keeps the conversation on track
- is unbiased

Focused Listening

As you listen, jot down specific key phrases the interviewer uses which reflect his responsibilities.

For Discussion

1. Why is poverty difficult to eliminate? What are some solutions Dr. Manders suggests?

2. Why do wealthy countries such as Canada rely heavily on food banks and other charitable organizations to feed their poor?

3. How could the media contribute towards reducing poverty in rich industrial countries?

Hunger is a problem in the wealthy industrialized countries such as Canada and the United States as well. Workers at a food bank pack supplies for families in need.

Speaking

Working in pairs, imagine, write, and present an interview between a news correspondent and one of the following:

- a fundraiser for UNICEF
- a food bank operator
- a local politician at election time
- a relief worker
- a homeless person

Unit Reflection

Working in teams of four or five, design a poster entitled "Food for Thought" which visually captures what you have learned in this unit.

Unit 10

The Circle of Life

DISCUSSION

1. What is the writer of the "Thought of the Day" below describing?
2. In your own words, describe the main characteristics of each of the four "seasons" of life.
3. What age ranges would you assign to the four "seasons" of life?
4. What connection do you see between the photographs and the "Thought of the Day?"

Thought of the Day

The question, "Which is the happiest season of life?" being referred to an aged man, he replied: "When spring comes, and in the soft air the buds are breaking on the trees, and they are covered with blossoms, I think, how beautiful is spring! And when the summer comes, and covers the trees with its heavy foliage, and singing birds are among the branches, I think, how beautiful is summer! When autumn loads them with golden fruit, and their leaves bear the gorgeous tint of frost, I think, how beautiful is autumn! And when it is sere winter, and there is neither foliage nor fruit, then I look up through the leafless branches, as I never could until now, and see the stars shine."

*- probably the Stoic philosopher
Seneca*

peaking

Many young children in English-speaking countries are introduced to the English nursery rhymes of Mother Goose very early on. The rhymes are very popular and children delight in repeating them over and over. In these short rhymes, animals can do extraordinary things. Everyday objects take on human qualities. The rhymes not only develop the imagination, but also good oral language skills as they are meant to be said aloud. Nursery rhymes are really a child's first introduction to poetry.

1. Below are six common nursery rhymes that have been separated into two parts. Match the rhymes in the boxes with their corresponding parts in the circles. Use rhyming and meaning to guide you. Then decide whether the box or the circle begins the rhyme.

A.

Hey diddle, diddle

The cat and the fiddle,

The cow jumped over the moon;

B.

Humpty Dumpty sat on a wall,

Humpty Dumpty had a great fall;

C.

There came a big spider,

Who sat down beside her

And frightened Miss Muffet away.

D.

" 'Tis time for all children

on the Earth

To think about getting to bed!"

E.

And broke his crown,

And Jill came tumbling after.

F.

Little Boy Blue,

Come blow your horn,

The sheep's in the meadow,

The cow's in the corn.

G.

All the King's horses and all the King's men

Couldn't put Humpty together again.

H.

Where is the boy

Who looks after the sheep?

He's under a haystack

Fast asleep.

I.

Jack and Jill

Went up the hill,

To fetch a pail of water;

Jack fell down,

J.

The man in the moon looked

out of the moon,

Looked out of the moon and said,

K.

Little Miss Muffet

Sat on a tuffet,

Eating her curds and whey;

L.

The little dog laughed

To see such sport,

And the dish ran away with the spoon.

2. Say the rhymes aloud and read them with a partner or group. Pay attention to the rhythm of the language.

3. Find all the words in the nursery rhymes that rhyme with the words below. Note that words do not have to be spelled the same to rhyme, e.g., bl*ue* and kn*ew*.

a) tune   d) grey

b) brown   e) dead

c) crawl

4. In small teams, write as many other rhyming words as you can for the words above within a set time limit. Share your words with other teams. Give your team one point for each word you have that no other team has.

Tip

In poetry, words that sound similar are acceptable for rhyming, e.g., moon and broom.

5. What letter combinations give you the vowel sounds below? Brainstorm as many words as possible with these sounds to find the letter combinations.

a) *uw* (spoon) –

b) *aw* (brown) –

c) *ey* (grey) –

d) *a* (crawl) –

e) *ɛ* (dead) –

6. Say these words. What vowel sound does each underlined letter combination make?

a) sl<u>eig</u>h   b) b<u>ough</u>t   c) l<u>eo</u>pard   d) sh<u>oe</u>

e) fil<u>et</u>

One Step Beyond

Children not only love rhyming songs and games, they also love stories. Like nursery rhymes, children's stories are meant to be told or read aloud. These stories not only reflect the values of society at the time in which they were written, but they also usually contain a lesson of life to be learned. One popular children's story in North America is "Little Red Riding Hood." In this story a young girl walks through the forest to visit her sick grandmother and bring her some good food to eat. Although warned not to speak to the big bad wolf on her way, Little Red Riding Hood is tricked by the disguised wolf and she and her grandmother are eventually eaten by the wolf. The lesson of the story is that appearances can be deceiving – you can't judge whether a person is bad by how he or she looks.

Tell a favourite or popular children's story from your native country. Create questions for your classmates that invite discussion about its meaning and lessons.

riting

Write a short children's story of your own creation that includes a lesson of life.

istening 1   T10.a

Before You Listen

In teams, discuss the following questions.

1. The scene above is from the dream of a young man. Do you think the scene is set in historical or modern times?

2. How might you interpret the meaning of the dream?

3. Do you think young people today can relate to the dream?

4. Think about how the parents in this scene are trying to raise the young man. Write down a few key words that come to mind when you look at this picture.

5. You are going to hear a poem titled, "Your Children Are Not Your Children." Based on the title and this dream scene, what messages do you think the poet might have?

Focused Listening

Some poetry is valued as representing universal, timeless truths. This poem, by the early twentieth-century poet Kahlil Gibran, is an example of such poetry. Listen to the poem and fill in the missing words.

Your Children Are Not Your Children

Your children are not your children,

They are the sons and daughters of Life's _____ for itself.

They _____ through you but not from you.

And though they are with you yet they _____ not to you.

You may _____ them your love but not your thoughts,

For they have their own thoughts.

You may _____ their bodies, but not their souls,

For their souls _____ in the house of tomorrow, which

   you cannot visit, even in your dreams.

You may _____ to be like them, but seek not to make them like you,

For life _____ not backward nor tarries with yesterday.

You are the bows from which your children as living arrows are _____ forth.

- Kahlil Gibran from *The Prophet* (1923)

For Discussion

1. In your own words, tell what this poet is saying.

2. What feelings do you associate with this poem?

3. Who is the target audience?

4. What does the poet mean when he says, "They came through you but not from you?"

5. The writer refers to some common mistakes parents make in raising their children. What are some of these mistakes? What do you think could be done to make parents realize some of their errors?

One Step Beyond

You will notice that the lines in this poem do not rhyme. This is an example of a prose poem. Nonetheless, the poem clearly sounds like poetry when read. What elements of language do you hear and see in this poem that make it poetry and not just "good advice?"

Choose one of the following titles and write a prose poem for an audience of young adults. Write in the same style as the Kahlil Gibran poem.

- In Your Parent's House You Shall Live Forever
- Your Parents Are Your Teachers
- A Parent's Advice Comes From The Heart

Reading 1

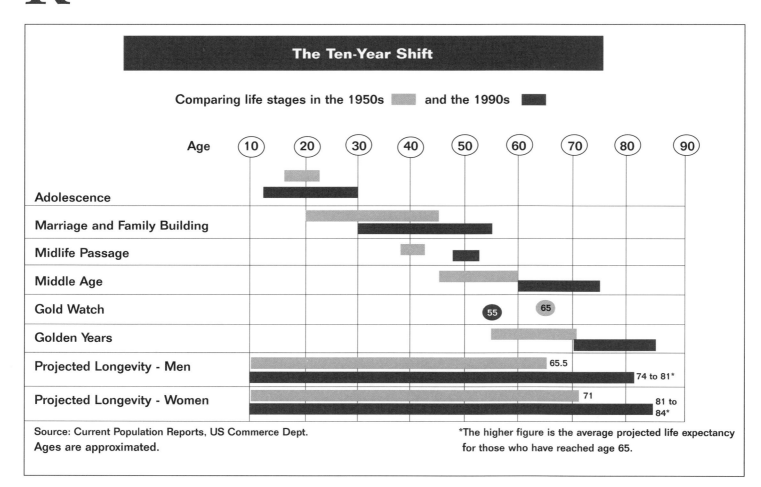

The Ten-Year Shift

Comparing life stages in the 1950s [ ] and the 1990s [ ]

Age	10	20	30	40	50	60	70	80	90

- Adolescence
- Marriage and Family Building
- Midlife Passage
- Middle Age
- Gold Watch — 55 / 65
- Golden Years
- Projected Longevity - Men — 65.5 / 74 to 81*
- Projected Longevity - Women — 71 / 81 to 84*

Source: Current Population Reports, US Commerce Dept.
Ages are approximated.

*The higher figure is the average projected life expectancy for those who have reached age 65.

Before You Read

1. Look at the graph above and discuss with a partner what the graph describes.

2. Based on information provided on the graph, what do you think "longevity" means?

3. You are about to read an article about the stages of human development. What information do you expect this reading to include?

A New Look At Human Development

The way we look at human development has changed dramatically over the last 100 years. Until the 1950s the study of human development was mainly concerned with identifying and defining the developmental stages of
5 childhood. In the 1950s however, Erik Erikson, an American psychologist, revolutionized the way we thought about human development by exploring stages of the human life cycle beyond childhood. According to Erikson, there were eight stages of human development,
10 including three stages in adult life: Young Adulthood, Maturity, and Old Age. The stages were regarded as steps on a ladder. Each step, he claimed, was ridden with conflicts that had to be resolved before a person could move to a higher stage.

15 Today, we have divided the stages of adult life even further. We constantly read about Baby Boomers, Generation Xers, pensioners, seniors, and the very old. The work of Gail Sheehy, another American writer on psychology, has contributed greatly to this further divi-
20 sion. In her 1995 book, *New Passages*, Sheehy writes that adulthood begins with the Pulling Up Roots stage, and continues through the Tryout Twenties, Turbulent Thirties, Flourishing Forties, Flaming Fifties, and Serene Sixties into old age.

25 What is fascinating about Sheehy's work is that she has gone beyond Erikson's theory. Whereas Erikson believed that a person had to come to terms with the conflicts of one life stage before going on to the next, and that life stages were associated with specific age ranges, Sheehy
30 theorizes that today, five generations, spanning birth dates from 1914 to 1980, occupy contemporary adulthood, and that there has been a significant shift in the age ranges that were traditionally associated with a particular life stage. Moreover, she claims that the ways in which people
35 deal with the tasks of each life stage are changing dramatically. For example, the World War II Generation (born 1914-1929) entered the Pulling Up Roots stage, a time when we strive to become independent of our parents, at about age 18 and usually completed it by age
40 22. This generation usually dealt with the tasks of this stage by getting married, and settling into some kind of job apprenticeship that led up the corporate ladder. Today, the Endangered Generation (born 1966 - 1980), referred to by some as Generation X, enters this same life

45 stage almost ten years later. Between the ages of 18 and 21, the Endangered Generation's main goal is to stay in school for as long as possible. Also, because of the changing workplace and economic environment, today's Generation Xers don't expect their careers to evolve in
50 the same ways as their parents' careers. Marriage is often delayed into their late twenties or even thirties. Many North American Generation Xers are skeptical about getting married at all, having grown up during a time when almost one out of two marriages ends in
55 divorce. Consequently this generation has to deal with the tasks of the Pulling Up Roots stage differently.[1]

Today's Generation Xers are getting married and having children later than their parents' generation.

It appears then that the traditional definitions and descriptions of life's stages do not apply to our times and most likely, that with continued globalization of cultures
60 and economies as well as new advances in technology and health care, the ages associated with specific life stages and how people tackle the conflicts of each stage will continue to be redefined in the future.

[1]Gail Sheehy, *New Passages: Mapping Your Life Across Time* (New York: Random House, Inc.), 1995.

---

(16) *Baby Boomers:* the generation that was born in the economic boom after World War II from about 1946 to 1960

(17) *pensioners:* people over the age of 65 who are retired

For Discussion

With a partner or in teams, discuss these questions.

1. What happened in the 1950s that revolutionized the study of human development?
2. Discuss three ways in which Gail Sheehy's theory of adult development differs from Erikson's theory.
3. What factors will affect how stages of adulthood will be defined in the future?

Organization

The sentences below are all from paragraphs in the article you have just read. They are not in the proper order. Without looking at the text, put the sentences into a logical order and rewrite the paragraph.

a) According to Erikson, there were eight stages of human development, including three stages in adult life: Young Adulthood, Maturity, and Old Age.
b) In the 1950s however, Erik Erikson, an American psychologist, revolutionized the way we thought about human development by exploring stages of the human life cycle beyond childhood.
c) The way we look at human development has changed dramatically over the last 100 years.
d) Each step, he claimed, was ridden with conflicts that had to be resolved before a person could move to a higher stage.
e) Until the 1950s the study of human development was mainly concerned with identifying and defining the developmental stages of childhood.
f) The stages were regarded as steps on a ladder.

One Step Beyond

1. According to the article, today's Generation Xers don't expect their careers to evolve in the same ways as their parents' careers did. How do you expect the careers of this generation to differ given today's technological, business, and economic environment?
2. Sheehy suggests that the Endangered Generation will have to deal with the Pulling Up Roots stage, a time when we strive to become independent of our parents, differently from previous generations. Why is this, and how do you think this generation will deal with the tasks of this stage?

Vocabulary 1

1. Guessing Meaning

Gail Sheehy has described various decades of adulthood as follows:

> *Tryout* Twenties
> *Turbulent* Thirties
> *Flourishing* Forties
> *Flaming* Fifties
> *Serene* Sixties

a) Based on your own experiences with people in these age groups, discuss what Sheehy means by each of these terms. Then, write the meaning of each adjective.

b) Discuss other uses of the adjectives. What nouns might you describe using these adjectives? Write a sentence for each adjective.

2. Word Forms

Learning new vocabulary is more than knowing the meaning of a word. You must learn to use a word in different grammatical forms. Copy and complete the chart on the next page. For each word:

a) find another grammatical form of the word in the reading
b) write a definition for the word based on its meaning in the sentence
c) list other forms of the word and identify their grammatical use.

The first one has been done for you.

Tip

When you learn a new word, be sure to learn its different meanings, possible grammatical forms, associated formality, and prepositions or other words that are often used with it.

Word	Form in Reading	Meaning	Other Forms
1. global	globalization "...with the continued globalization of cultures and economies..."	the process of spreading across the world	globe *(n)* global *(adj)* globally *(adv)* globalize *(v)*
2. revolution			
3. apprentice			
4. develop			
5. mature			
6. theory			

3. Formality Register

The article you read is an example of academic writing and has a formal tone. One way to achieve this tone is to use formal vocabulary. Find the words below (or forms of them) in the reading and write an informal equivalent for each one. Use a thesaurus if you need help.

a) strive

b) contemporary

c) span

d) resolve

e) evolve

TENSE REVIEW

1. Tenses in English

In English we categorize events according to time perspectives. There are three time perspectives:

1. Past

2. Present/No specific time

3. Future

We help the listener or reader understand our time perspective by using verb tenses (verb forms that show time). We can also use time expressions, such as *yesterday, last month, tomorrow,* or *in ten years.* Usually we combine verb tense and time expressions.

Tip

Be careful not to confuse time and tense. Tenses are verb forms that show time relationships.

2. Choosing Tense

The first step in determining which tense to use in any situation is to identify the time perspective: Past, Present/No specific time, or Future. For example, the primary time frame of the article "A New Look At Human Development" is the present. The writer's main point is that the stages of human development, specifically adult development, are being redefined. Think of time perspective as three signs under which you stand when you speak.

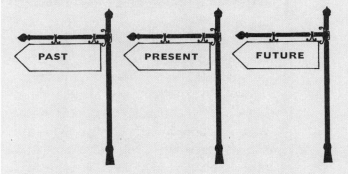

In the reading, "A New Look At Human Development," the writer is primarily standing under the Present/No specific time position.

Grammar Focus

3. No Specific Time

Sometimes we are not really referring to a specific time. Rather, we are speaking about something in which the time is not important, or not specific.

EXAMPLE: Water boils at 100°C.

In this sentence, we are not referring to yesterday, now, or tomorrow. This is a *general truth*. Much scientific information falls into this category.

EXAMPLE: In her 1995 book, *New Passages*, Sheehy writes that adulthood begins with the Pulling Up Roots stage.

Again, this statement is not time specific. It refers to a situation that is generally true. When we speak of general truths or things that do not have a specific time frame, we use simple present tense.

Exercise A

Read the following paragraphs and identify the main time perspective of each passage. Each paragraph will have only one main time perspective: P (Past), Pr (Present), F (Future), or NST (No specific time).

1. ☐ Grandfather loved to tell stories of his childhood on the farm. He once told me of a time when he was seven. He had been playing with his friends when his brother dared him to ride one of the horses bareback. Confident in his own riding ability, he accepted the challenge. When he lost control of the horse, however, he rode right through his mother's laundry line.

2. ☐ In the future there will be lots of work, but few jobs. Freelance and consulting work will be common work patterns for many people. Young people entering the workforce in 20 years will have to arm themselves with a different set of skills than those of their predecessors because they will be bidding for work instead of attending job interviews. They will not only have to have job-related skills, but will also have to be able to sell themselves, work independently, and be self-motivating. Luckily for me, I will already have retired by that time.

3. ☐ One of the most interesting areas of brain research proves that early stimulation of the infant and child brain has significant effects on later intellectual development. For example, researchers have found that children who learn to read and play musical instruments at a young age eventually do better in mathematics than children who do not receive music training. The sets of neurons in the brain that develop with music training are the same sets of neurons that are involved in calculating mathematical problems. Consequently, the neurons used when doing mathematics are better developed in children who have received early music training.

4. ☐ Mother is washing the dishes again. I watch her from the dinner table, now cleared of dirty plates, grimy glasses, and left-over meatloaf. The steam from the hot, soapy water rises. As she rinses a glass, I see her hands, red and swollen. How many dishes have those hands washed? How many meals have they cooked, these hands that tell a life story? How many shirts have those hands ironed? How many dirty socks have those fingers turned right-side-out? How many soiled diapers have those hands changed? How many scraped knees have they cleansed and bandaged? How many tears have they wiped? With these thoughts still racing through my mind I get up slowly, grab a dish towel and help – because I am a good daughter.

5. ☐ I'm going home next spring. As soon as I get there I'm going to call my best friend Tanja. By then we won't have seen each other for a whole year. Then we're going to go to all the spots where we used to hang out: the clubs, the shops, and our special swimming spot along the river. It'll be great.

Exercise B

Read the paragraphs on the previous page again and identify the verbs in each sentence. Using a chart like the one below, try to identify the specific tenses of all the verbs in each paragraph.

Past Perspective		Present/No Specific Time	Future Perspective
1. *loved*	simple past		
told	simple past		
had been playing	past perfect progressive		
etc.			

4. Tense Considerations

There are two points to consider when deciding which tense to use:

- the time when an action occurs
- the characteristics (meaning) of that action

For example, the progressive *ing* form of a verb gives meaning to the action. It tells us that the action is in progress (not finished) or temporary.

EXAMPLES: Peter is giving a speech.
(action in progress)

Helga is studying law.
(temporary action)

We can think of actions as having four possible characteristics. An action is:

1. *at* that time
2. *in progress during* that time
3. *before* that time
4. *in progress during and before* that time

Using this model, consider the tense chart below. According to the chart, past progressive means an event that was in progress (not finished) during some time in the past. (For a complete review of tenses and meanings in all four time perspectives, see the Appendix on page 160).

The English Tense System

Meaning/ Time	Simple (at that time)	Progressive (in progress during that time)	Perfect (before that time)	Perfect Progressive (in progress during and before that time)
Present				
Past				
Future				

* Note: Don't forget that we use simple present tense to talk about actions of no specific time.

Grammar Focus

Exercise C

The sentences below are in different tenses. Identify the tense of the main verb and discuss why it is used. Then, decide where the sentence fits in the tense chart on the previous page.

1. Generation Xers enter the Pulling Up Roots stage almost ten years later than the World War II Generation.

2. Erikson revolutionized the way we thought about human development.

3. For centuries, philosophers have been trying to understand how people change over the course of their lives.

4. In the mid-seventies, psychologists at the University of California were studying how people's lives change during young and middle adulthood.

5. She had always considered herself a mature adult until the birth of her first child.

6. The definitions of life's stages will continue to be redefined in the future.

7. The way we look at human development has changed dramatically over the last 100 years.

8. People now in their thirties are complaining that they will be left to clean up the economic mess their parents' and grandparents' generations have created.

9. By the year 2005 the number of people between the ages of 40 and 49 will have increased by about one million compared to 1995.

10. In the future, advertisers will no longer be targeting the youth market.

11. Until the 1950s psychologists had been concentrating their efforts on defining the stages of childhood.

12. These days, by the time many couples get married, they will likely have been living together for at least one year.

Grammar In Use

The education ministry is concerned about the drop-out rate of students going from elementary to high school and from high school to college/university. The ministry wants to increase students' success rates by easing the transition from one level to the next. You have been invited to participate in a panel discussion to share your personal experiences. In teams, choose one of the following:

- a panel discussion for an audience of elementary school graduates who are going to enter high school next year

- a panel discussion for an audience of high school graduates who are going on to college/university

Assume you will be asked questions by students in the audience. Anticipate eight questions your panel may be asked. For example, you may be asked to describe your first day of high school or college/university. Prepare answers to these questions and present your panel discussion for the class.

Listening 2

T10.b

You will hear four short interviews with people of different ages: Christopher, an 8-year-old boy in grade three; Serene, a 17-year-old girl in her last year of high school; Martha, a 40-year-old mother of two; and Konrad, an 86-year-old man. They were all asked the same questions about their lives.

Before You Listen

Work individually or in teams. Choose one of the characters who is not in your own age group and answer the questions below from that age group's perspective. Then share your answers with classmates who chose a different age group.

1. What do you enjoy doing in your spare time?

2. What kinds of things frighten you or worry you at this stage in your life?

3. What's the best thing about being a person your age?

4. What's the worst thing about being a person your age?

5. What is the most important thing or who are the most important people in your life at this time?

6. What do you want to tell younger people about people your age?

7. What do you want to tell older people about people your age?

Focused Listening

Now listen to the interviews and note each character's answers in point form.

Comprehension Check

1. Compare your notes with a partner.

2. Discuss the differences and similarities between your predicted answers and the characters' interview answers. Discuss at least two responses that surprised you.

One Step Beyond

1. The dialogues you have just heard are transcripts from authentic interviews. Listen again to each interview and compare how each character uses language and tone of voice differently to communicate.

2. How have values and what is important changed from previous generations? Imagine that four people in the same age groups as the ones in this listening exercise had been asked these questions in the late 1930s. How would their answers be different from the ones you just heard?

Christopher (8 years old)

Serene (17 years old)

Konrad
(86 years old)

Martha (40 years old)

riting

Imagine yourself at 80 years old. Write about what kind of person you will be, what you hope your life will be like, and what you hope to have achieved.

Speaking

What do you want future generations to know about you? In teams, create a time capsule, collecting items that will show future generations the values and concerns of young adults at the dawn of the new millennium (the year 2000). Explain what future generations will say about you based on your time capsule.

Reading 2

According to *Washington Magazine*, Robert Fulghum "is a storyteller who can pluck at your heartstrings, tickle your funny bone, and point up a moral all at the same time." You will read one of his narrative essays that reflects on an aspect of family life and on life stages from his #1 Bestseller *It Was On Fire When I Lay Down On It*.

Before You Read

1. Think of some personal items you have collected over the years that you will not throw away because of their sentimental value. Share some of these with your classmates.

2. Think of five items a 7-year-old boy might collect to keep in a personal treasure box. What about a 7-year-old girl?

The Cardboard Box Is Marked "The Good Stuff"

1 As I write, I can see the box where it is stored on a high shelf in my studio. I like being able to see it when I look up. The box contains those odds and ends of personal treasures that have survived many bouts of clean-it-out-and-throw-it-away that seize me from time to time. The box has passed through the screening done as I've moved from house to house and hauled stuff from attic to attic. A thief looking into the box would not take anything – he couldn't get a dime for any of it. But if the house ever catches on fire, the box goes with me when I run.

2 One of the keepsakes in the box is a small paper bag. Lunch size. Though the top is sealed with duct tape, staples, and several paper clips, there is a ragged rip in one side through which the contents may be seen.

3 This particular lunch sack has been in my care for maybe fourteen years. But it really belongs to my daughter, Molly. Soon after she came of school age, she became an enthusiastic participant in packing the morning lunches for herself, her brothers, and me. Each bag got a share of sandwiches, apples, milk money, and sometimes a note or a treat. One morning, Molly handed me two bags as I was about to leave. One regular lunch sack. And the one with the duct tape and staples and paper clips. "Why two bags?" "The other one is something else." "What's in it?" "Just some stuff – take it with you." Not wanting to hold court over the matter, I stuffed both sacks into my briefcase, kissed the child, and rushed off.

4 At midday, while hurriedly scarfing down my real lunch, I tore open Molly's bag and shook out the contents. Two hair ribbons, three small stones, a plastic dinosaur, a pencil stub, a tiny seashell, two animal crackers, a marble, a used lipstick, a small doll, two chocolate kisses, and thirteen pennies.

5 I smiled. How charming. Rising to hustle off to all the important business of the afternoon, I swept the desk clean - into the wastebasket - leftover lunch, Molly's junk, and all. There wasn't anything in there I needed.

6 That evening Molly came to stand beside me while I was reading the paper. "Where's my bag?" "What bag?" "You know, the one I gave you this morning." "I left it at the office, why?" "I forgot to put this note in it." She hands over the note. "Besides, I want it back."

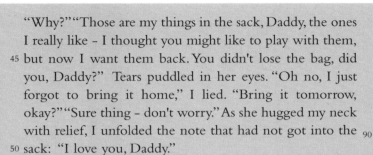
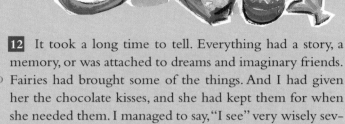

"Why?" "Those are my things in the sack, Daddy, the ones I really like - I thought you might like to play with them, but now I want them back. You didn't lose the bag, did you, Daddy?" Tears puddled in her eyes. "Oh no, I just forgot to bring it home," I lied. "Bring it tomorrow, okay?" "Sure thing - don't worry." As she hugged my neck with relief, I unfolded the note that had not got into the sack: "I love you, Daddy."

7 Oh.
And also – uh-oh.
I looked long at the face of my child.
She was right – what was in that sack was
"something else."

8 Molly had given me her treasures. All that a seven-year-old held dear. Love in a paper sack. And I had missed it. Not only missed it, but had thrown it in the waste-basket because "there wasn't anything in there I needed." Dear God.

9 It wasn't the first time or the last time I felt my Daddy Permit was about to run out.

10 It was a long trip back to the office. But there was nothing else to be done. So I went. The pilgrimage of a penitent. Just ahead of the janitor, I picked up the waste-basket and poured the contents on my desk. I was sorting it all out when the janitor came in to do his chores. "Lose something?" "Yeah, my mind." "It's probably in there, all right. What's it look like and I'll help you find it?" I started not to tell him. But I couldn't feel any more of a fool than I was already in fact, so I told him. He didn't laugh. He smiled. "I got kids, too." So the brotherhood of fools searched the trash and found the jewels and he smiled at me and I smiled at him. You are never alone in these things. Never.

11 After washing the mustard off the dinosaurs and spraying the whole thing with breath-freshener to kill the smell of onions, I carefully smoothed out the wadded ball of brown paper into a semifunctional bag and put the trea-sures inside and carried the whole thing home gingerly, like an injured kitten. The next evening I returned it to Molly, no questions asked, no explanations offered. The bag didn't look so good, but the stuff was all there and that's what counted. After dinner I asked her to tell me about the stuff in the sack, and so she took it all out a piece at a time and placed the objects in a row on the dining room table.

12 It took a long time to tell. Everything had a story, a memory, or was attached to dreams and imaginary friends. Fairies had brought some of the things. And I had given her the chocolate kisses, and she had kept them for when she needed them. I managed to say, "I see" very wisely sev-eral times in the telling. And as a matter of fact, I did see.

13 To my surprise, Molly gave the bag to me once again several days later. Same ratty bag. Same stuff inside. I felt forgiven. And trusted. And loved. And a little more com-fortable wearing the title of Father. Over several months the bag went with me from time to time. It was never clear to me why I did or did not get it on a given day. I began to think of it as the Daddy Prize and tried to be good the night before so I might be given it the next morning.

14 In time Molly turned her attention to other things . . . found other treasures . . . lost interest in the game . . . grew up. Something. Me? I was left holding the bag. She gave it to me one morning and never asked for its return. And so I have it still.

15 Sometimes I think of all the times in this sweet life when I must have missed the affection I was being given. A friend calls this "standing knee-deep in the river and dying of thirst."

16 So the worn paper sack is in the box. Left over from a time when a child said, "Here - this is the best I've got. Take it - it's yours. Such as I have, give I to thee."

17 I missed it the first time. But it's my bag now.

---

(3) *odds and ends:* various small items that usually don't have much value
(5) *seize:* take hold of
(11) *keepsake:* something you keep because it holds special memories for you
(12) *duct tape:* a special strong tape designed to hold pipes together
(13) *ragged:* uneven
(28) *scarfing:* eating quickly
(78) *wadded:* pressed tightly together
(80) *gingerly:* carefully
(105) *to be left holding the bag:* to have final responsibility

Comprehension Check

1. To find the answers to the questions below, scan the paragraphs indicated in the numbered boxes.

   a) In your own words, tell what two things make the box on the shelf special. **1**
   b) What did each family member's lunch bag contain? **3**
   c) What food items were in the paper bag? **4**
   d) What lie did the father tell his daughter? **6**
   e) What did the father say to his daughter when he returned the bag? **11**
   f) How did the father know the daughter still trusted him? **13**

2. This story contains a lot of information that isn't necessary to understanding the "key" actions, but that helps create the "feeling" of the story. Identify the essential information that tells the actions in the story. Then summarize the story in one paragraph using the W5H question format as a guide: Who, What, Where, When, Why, and How.

For Discussion

The real purpose of this story is not to tell what happened to the father. It is to send a broader message — to make a statement about being a parent. What phrase in the story would you say reveals the "key" message the writer wants to leave us with?

One Step Beyond

1. The tone of this reading is very different from the tone of "A New Look At Human Development." Describe and compare the styles of the two readings. Then note what language and literary strategies contribute to the tone of each.

2. In paragraph 16 the writer uses the sentence: "Such as I have, give I to thee." What strikes you as unusual about this sentence and why has the writer used this element?

Writing

Write a narrative essay. Tell a story about a simple event that happened to you or someone you know illustrating an important point about a specific stage of life.

Unit Reflection

The title of this unit is "The Circle of Life." Create your own circle of life. Draw a large circle on a blank sheet. Divide the circle into eight parts. Choose one part to begin the process outlined below, then continue around the circle.

1. Write the date and place of your birth. Write a few key words that describe where you were born.

2. List your favourite foods as a young child.

3. Write something important you remember learning as a child.

4. Write the title of a book or movie that made a strong impression on you as a teen.

5. Write the name of a famous person you admired as a young teen.

6. Write your ideal occupation.

7. Write three things you plan to have achieved by the time you are 35 years old.

8. Write three adjectives that describe the kind of person you want to be when you are 85 years old.

Now work in teams and discuss the circle of your life with your teammates.

Unit 2

Reading 2 *Your Astrological Sign*

a) Taurus (the bull)
b) Cancer (the crab)
c) Virgo (the virgin)
d) Libra (the scales)
e) Sagittarius (the archer)
f) Aquarius (the water bearer)
g) Aries (the ram)
h) Gemini (the twins)
i) Leo (the lion)
j) Scorpio (the scorpion)
k) Capricorn (the goat)
l) Pisces (the fish)

Unit 3

Travel Quiz *Where in the World is Marco?*

1. Ayers Rock in Australia
2. The Grand Canyon in Arizona, USA
3. Stonehenge in England
4. The Colosseum in Rome, Italy
5. Anne of Green Gables house on Prince Edward Island, Canada
6. The Taj Mahal in India
7. The Statue of Liberty in New York City, USA
8. The Great Wall of China
9. The Great Pyramids in Egypt
10. Angel Falls in Venezuela, South America

Unit 6

Reading 1 *Are You a Genius?*

1. His son. Draw a box and label it Bill. Draw another box for his mother-in-law and connect them. Draw a third box for his mother-in-law's only daughter, who has to be Bill's wife. Then a fourth box for her son, who also has to be Bill's son.

2. Twenty-seven. Each number has three times the value of the number preceding it.

3. c) A general knowledge question.

4. My friend the test pilot was named Susan. Did you assume the pilot was male?

5. Ten. In the rear corner, the stack is three high, but you can only see the top one. The second row is two high, with a supporting block hidden under each.

6. REFRIGERATOR

7. Jennifer is 15, in a system that awards five points for each syllable in the name.

8. Twenty-four.

9. c) Cave. All the others are human-made.

10. Twenty

11. HAND

12. Four girls and three boys.

13. b) J. The letters are the first letters of the months of the year, beginning with January.

14. Eyelid is to eye as curtain is to window.

15. PEOPLE WHO LIVE IN GLASS HOUSES SHOULD NOT THROW STONES.

16. (D) Here you need only check for the white ring on one side and the three-dot triangle on the other.

17. ATTACK AT DAWN MONDAY. The lieutenant lifted the first letter out of each word and strung the letters together.

18. KNOWLEDGE IS POWER.

19. Six. The first number on each line is divided by the second to give the third.

20. (D) The outer figure rotates clockwise by quarter turns; the line moves from left side to right side and back again; the smaller figure rotates counterclockwise by quarter turns.

Unit 6

Reading 2 *Who Murdered Ellington Breese?*

1. Walters, the nephew, murdered Ellington Breese.

2. The police deduced that Walters was the murderer from the fact that the flies and the mosquitos found dead were on the window sill instead of around the room. This indicated that the gas had spread through the room after dawn, for the following reasons: a poison gas, powerful enough to kill a human being, would kill instantly such insects as flies and mosquitos. Therefore, they must have been at the windows when overtaken by the gas. From this it can be deduced that it was light at the time, since such insects, in a dark room, are attracted to the windows by the light coming in beneath partially drawn blinds. It may be logically considered to be very improbable that the flies would all have been found on the window sills had the instantaneously fatal gas been released in the darkness of the night. Observation of this clue led the detectives to another questioning of Walters, who eventually broke down and confessed to the crime. He had stolen down at the break of dawn. He had lost a substantial amount of money through speculation, it was later discovered, and this had driven Walters to the deed. He was subsequently convicted and executed early in 1926.

Unit 6

Grammar Focus 2 - *Grammar In Use*

Miss White is wearing black.
Miss Black is wearing gray.
Miss Gray is wearing white.

Unit 8

Reading 2 *Athletes Matching*

1. f	6. h
2. i	7. c
3. a	8. g
4. d	9. e
5. b	10. j

Vocabulary 2

1. a) by a nose
   b) hole in one
   c) bull's eye
   d) quarterback
   e) forward
   f) heavyweight
   g) right guard
   h) greatest
   i) pitcher
   j) tennis pro
   k) goalie

Unit 9

Reading 1 *Shopper's Quiz*

1. b
2. a
3. c
4. a
5. b
6. c
7. b
8. a

Unit 6

Listening 1 *Tapescript*

Martin Luther King Jr.'s Speech (Alabama 1955)

(First Segment) We're here this evening for serious business. We're here in a general sense because first and foremost, we are American citizens, and we are determined to acquire our citizenship to the fullness of its meaning. We are here also because of our deep-seated belief that democracy transformed from thin paper to thick action is the greatest form of government on earth.

(Second Segment) There comes a time that people get tired. We are here this evening to say to those who have mistreated us so long that we are tired — tired of being segregated and humiliated; tired of being kicked about by the brutal feet of oppression.

There comes a time my friends when people get tired of being plunged across the abyss of humiliation, when they experience the bleakness of nagging despair. There comes a time when people get tired of being pushed out of the glimmering sunlight of last July and left standing amid the piercing chill of an Alpine November.

(Third Segment) We had no alternative but to protest. For many years, we have shown amazing patience. We have sometimes given our white brothers the feeling that we liked the way we were being treated. But we come here tonight to be saved from that patience that makes us patient with anything less than freedom and justice.

One of the great glories of democracy is the right to protest for right.

(Fourth Segment) These organizations (White Citizens' Councils and the Ku Klux Klan) are protesting for the perpetuation of injustice in the community; we are protesting for the birth of justice in the community. Their methods lead to violence and lawlessness. But in our protest there will be no cross burnings. No white person will be taken from his home by a hooded Negro mob and brutally murdered. There will be no threats and intimidation. We will be guided by the highest principles of law and order.

Our method will be that of persuasion, not coercion. We will only say to the people, "Let your conscience be your guide." Our actions must be guided by the deepest principles of our Christian faith. Love must be our regulating ideal. Once again we must hear the words of Jesus echoing across the centuries ("Love your enemies, bless them that curse you, and pray for them that despitefully use you"). If we fail to do this our protest will end up as a meaningless drama on the stage of history, and its memory will be shrouded with the ugly garments of shame. In spite of the mistreatment that we have confronted we must not become bitter, and end up by hating our white brothers. As Booker T. Washington said, "Let no man pull you so low as to make you hate him."

(Fifth Segment) We are not wrong in what we are doing. If we are wrong, the Supreme Court of this nation is wrong. If we are wrong, the Constitution of the United States is wrong. If we are wrong, God Almighty is wrong. If we are wrong, Jesus of Nazareth was merely a Utopian dreamer who never came down to earth.

(Sixth Segment) If you will protest courageously, and yet with dignity and Christian love, when the history books are written in future generations, the historians will have to pause and say, "There lived a great people — a black people — who injected new meaning and dignity into the veins of civilization." This is our challenge and our overwhelming responsibility.

Grammar Appendix

Grammar Focus 1

Common reporting verbs:

add	complain	point out
admit	deny	promise
answer	explain	protest
argue	remark	object
observe	reply	remind + object
yell	shout	tell + object

Unit 2

Grammar Focus 2

Common verbs of inquiry:

inquire	wonder	want to know	ask

Unit 5

Grammar Focus 1

Mental activity verbs commonly followed by a noun clause beginning with *that:*

acknowledge	find (wh)	recommend
admit	forget (wh)	remark
advise	guarantee	remember (wh)
agree	happen	remind
allege	hear (wh)	request
announce	hope	resolve
appear	imagine (wh)	reveal (wh)
arrange (wh)	imply	say (wh)
ask (wh)	indicate (wh)	see (wh)
assume	inform	seem
assure	insist	show (wh)
beg	know (wh)	state (wh)
believe (wh)	learn	stipulate
command	make out (= state)	suggest (wh)
confess	mean	suppose
consider (wh)	notice (wh)	teach
declare	observe	tell (wh)
decide (wh)	occur to + object	think (wh)
demand	order	threaten
demonstrate	perceive	turn out
determine	presume	understand (wh)
discover	pretend	urge
doubt	promise	vow
estimate (wh)	propose	warn
expect	prove (wh)	wish
fear	realize (wh)	wonder (wh)
feel	recognize	

Verbs marked (wh) can also be followed by noun clauses beginning with "wh" words.

Grammar Focus

Common verbs that are followed by the *to + base* verbal or infinitive:

agree	forget	prepare
arrange	hesitate	pretend
ask	hope	promise
attempt	intend	refuse
choose	manage	volunteer
decide	neglect	wish
demand	offer	
deserve	plan	

Unit 8

Grammar Focus 1

Verbs followed by the *base + ing* verbal (gerund):

admit	loathe
anticipate	mean (= involve)
appreciate	mind (= object)
avoid	miss
consider	pardon
defer	postpone
delay	practise
deny	prevent
detest	propose (= suggest)
dislike	recollect
dread	remember (= recollect)
enjoy	resent
escape	resist
excuse	risk
fancy (= imagine)	save (somebody the
finish	trouble of)
forgive	stop (= cease)
imagine	suggest
involve	understand
keep (= continue)	

Grammar Focus

Verb Tenses in English

Tense	Use	Example
Simple Present	1. general statements of fact/no specific time	Reading is fun.
	2. habitual, everyday activities	I read the newspaper every morning.
	3. verbs not used in continuous forms (e.g., *be, hear, love*, etc.)	I love to read.
	4. schedules	The library opens at 9:00 a.m.
Present Progressive	1. activity in progress when speaking	I am reading.
	2. ongoing activity	I am reading a great novel.
Present Perfect	1. activity that happened at an unspecified time in the past (where the action is important, not the exact time)	I have read that book before.
	2. activity that was repeated in the past and could be again	I have read that book many times.
	3. activity that began in the past and continues to the present	I have worked at this library for three years.
Present Perfect Progressive	1. emphasis on the **duration** of an activity that began in the past and continues to the present	I have been reading for two hours.
	2. general activity in progress recently	I have been reading a lot of science fiction novels recently.
Simple Past	1. activity that began and finished at a specific time in the past	I read that chapter last night.
Past Progressive	1. past activity that was in progress when it was interrupted by another action in the past	I was reading when the phone rang.
	2. past activity that was in progress (used to describe a background scene)	It was a quiet afternoon. Mom and Dad were reading.
	3. past activity that was in progress for a time	I was reading.
	4. past activities that were in progress during the same period	I was reading and John was listening to his favourite CD.

Tense	Use	Example
Past Perfect	1. past activity that was completed before another event/time	I had already read that book before it was assigned.
Past Perfect Progressive	1. emphasis on the **duration** of a past activity that was in progress before and up to another past event/time	I had been reading Shakespeare before I started high school.
	2. past activity that was in progress recent to but not until another past event/time	I had just been reading that book when it was assigned.
Simple Future (*will*)	Future events that emphasize:	
	1. statement of fact	The new book will be available in bookstores next month.
	2. prediction	The movie star's new book will be very popular.
	3. determination	Despite my lack of education I will learn to read.
	4. willingness	I will lend you my copy of the book.
	5. promise	I will return the book tomorrow.
Simple Future (*be going to*)	Future events that involve:	
	1. plan	I am going to read that book next week.
	2. prediction	People are always going to read books.
Future Progressive (*will/be going to*)	1. activity in progress at a time in the future	I will be reading during my holidays.
Future Perfect (*will/be going to*)	1. future activity that will be completed before another future event/time	I will have read the first chapter by the end of next week.
Future Perfect Progressive (*will/be going to*)	1. emphasis on the **duration** of an activity that will be in progress before another future event/time	I will have been working at the library for six years by the end of January.

Abbreviations
r = right
l = left
c = centre
t = top
b = bottom

Archive = Archive Photos
Bettmann = Corbis-Bettmann
Granger = The Granger Collection, New York
Kobal = Kobal Collection

1 (t, r) Reuters/Bettmann, (b) Warren Faidley/Picture Group/Publiphoto, (l)AP/Fort Morgan Times/Don Lassiter/Canapress; 2 (b) Stephen Dupont/Canapress, (cl) Reuters/Bettmann, (tl) Gordon Girradd/Science Photo Library/Publiphoto; 3 Greg Vaughn/Tony Stone; 8 Collection of the Department of Indian and Northern Affairs Canada; 14 Bill Becker/Canapress; 20 Bettmann; 30 (tr) Pat Morrow/First Light, (br) Atalante/Ponpresse, (bl) Boston Public Library, (cl) Galaxy Contact/Explorer/Publiphoto, (tl) World Perspective/Explorer/Publiphoto; 31 (tr) First Light, (br) Granger, (cl) P. Hattenberger/Publiphoto, (tl) Granger; 32 Corel-CDROM, 33 (tr) Jean Guichard/Sygma/Publiphoto, (br) M. Renaudeau/Hoa-Qui/Publiphoto, (bc) Doug Boult/Tony Stone, (tc) Corel CDROM, (bl) Ken Fisher/Tony Stone, (tl) Corel CDROM; 35 (t) P. Quittemelle/Publiphoto, (b) John Sylvester/First Light, (l) Cosmo Condina/Tony Stone; 37 Courtesy Don Starkell; 39 Granger; 43 Maitland Rapids on the Rideau River by JP Cockburn/Courtesy of the Royal Ontario Museum/942.4810; 44/ National Archives of Canada/C-7043; 45 Photo by Jack Hamilton/United Church Observer; 46 Galaxy Contact/Explorer/Publiphoto; 48 S. Villerot/Diaf/Publiphoto; 50 (l) Skjold Photos, (r) Eric R. Berndt/Unicorn Stock Photos; 53 Natalie Cajic/Seneca College; 60 George White/First Light; 62 (bl) Granger, (tr) Art Resource; 63 (c) Granger; (b) Scala/Art Resource; 65 (l) Kobal Collection; (r) Paramount (Courtesy Kobal); 69 Paramount (Courtesy Kobal); 71 Photo Researchers, Inc.; 73 Archive/Jeff J. Mitchell/Reuters; 77 Mehau Kulyk/Science Photo Library/Publiphoto; 80 Mehau Kulyk/Science Photo Library/Publiphoto; 85 (tr) Archive/Popperfoto, (cr) Bettmann, (br) The Image Works, (bl) UPI/Bettmann, (cb) Reuters/Bettmann, (ct) Archive/American Stock, (tl) Ponopresse; 86 Archive/American Stock; 94 (tr) Paramount/Courtesy Kobal, (br) Archive/CBS Photo Archives, (bl) UPI/Bettmann; 95 (tr) Ponopresse, (cr) Kobal, (br) Granger, (bl) Archive/American Stock, (cl) Heather Delfino, (tl) UPI/Bettmann; 97 (t) Archive, (b) Archive/Popperfoto; 104 Archive/Express Newspapers; 107 Archive/TM & © 20th Century Fox Film Corp./1991; 110 Archive/Michael Barson Collection; 111 (tr) Schuster/Publiphoto, (cr) Gloria McPherson, (br) Reuters/Bettmann, (bl) AFB/Bettmann, (cl) Jean-Marc Charles/Sygma/Publiphoto; 113 Bettmann; 114 Roger McPherson; 115 Julien Lama/Publiphoto; 117 Roger McPherson; 121 Scala/Art Resource; 126 (tr) Gamma/Ponopresse, (br) Jeff Greenberg/Unicorn Stock Photos, (bl) Dick Hemingway, (cl) Lawrence Misdale/Tony Stone; 127 (tr, br, bl) Rick Brady, (tl) National Eating Disorders Centre, 200 Elizabeth St., Toronto; 129 Rick Brady; 130 Andrew Sacks/Tony Stone; 133 (l) National Eating Disorders Information Centre, 200 Elizabeth St., Toronto, (r) UPI/Bettmann; 136 D&J Heaton/First Light; 137 Reuters/Bettmann; 140 Hans Deryk/Canapress; 141 (t) PH Royer/Explorer/Publiphoto, (cr) Rouchon/Explorer/Publiphoto, (cl) BSIP Keene/Publiphoto, (b) JY Derome/Publiphoto; 147 Cleo Freelance Photography; 153 (r) Heather Delfino, (b) Cleo Freelance Photography, (cl) Dick Hemingway.